BUFFALO BILL
AND HIS
WILD WEST

BUFFALO BILL
AND HIS
WILD WEST
A Pictorial Biography

Joseph G. Rosa and Robin May

UNIVERSITY PRESS OF KANSAS

© 1989 by the University Press of Kansas

Published by the University Press of Kansas
(Lawrence, Kansas 66045), which was organized
by the Kansas Board of Regents and is operated
and funded by Emporia State University, Fort
Hays State University, Kansas State University,
Pittsburg State University, the University of
Kansas, and Wichita State University

Printed in the United States of America
10 9 8 7 6 5 4 3 2 1
This book is printed on acid-free paper.

Library of Congress Cataloging-in-Publication
Data
Rosa, Joseph G.
  Buffalo Bill and his wild West : a pictorial
biography / Joseph G. Rosa and Robin May.
    p. cm.
    Bibliography: p.
    Includes index.
    ISBN 0-7006-0398-0 (alk. paper)
  ISBN 0-7006-0399-9 (pbk. : alk. paper)
    1. Buffalo Bill, 1846–1917—Pictorial works.
2. Pioneers—West (U.S.)—Biography—
Pictorial works. 3. Scouts and scouting—West
(U.S.)—Biography—Pictorial works. 4.
Entertainers—United States—Biography—
Pictorial works. 5. West (U.S.)—Biography—
Pictorial works. 6. Buffalo Bill's Wild West and
Pawnee Bill's Great Far East (Show)—History—
Pictorial works. I. May, Robin. II. Title.
F594.B63R67   1989
978'.02'0924—dc19
[B]   88-34426
                                                      CIP

British Library Cataloguing-in-Publication Data
is available

CONTENTS

By Joseph G. Rosa

They Called Him Wild Bill: The Life and Adventures of James Butler Hickok (Norman, Okla., 1964 and 1974)
Alias Jack McCall (Kansas City, Mo., 1967)
The Gunfighter: Man or Myth? (Norman, Okla., 1969)
Colonel Colt London (London, 1976)
The West of Wild Bill Hickok (Norman, Okla., 1982)
Guns of the American West (London, 1985)
Colt Revolvers and the Tower of London (London, 1988)

With Robin May

The Pleasure of Guns (London, 1974)
Gunsmoke: A Study of Violence in the Wild West (London, 1977—published in the United States as *Gun Law: A Study of Violence in the Wild West*—Chicago, 1977)

By Robin May

Wolfe's Army (London, 1974)
The Gold Rushes (London and New York, 1978)
The Story of the Wild West (London and New York, 1985)

With Joseph G. Rosa

Cowboy: The Man and the Myth (London, 1980)

PREFACE

William Frederick Cody, alias "Buffalo Bill," did more than anyone to promote the myths and the reality of the frontier West. His Wild West exhibition enthralled thousands of people the world over. Its colorful scenes depicting events and characters of a fast-fading era—already a legend—captivated audiences wherever it appeared, and its impact, especially in England, is remembered a century later. Cody's success is made even more remarkable by the fact that he was a man of humble origins who progressed from "prairie to palace" in less than twenty years following a varied career as a plains scout turned actor and showman.

Buffalo Bill's reputation, like that of some of his contemporaries, has suffered at the hands of "revisionists," to say nothing of debunkers whose conclusions are not supported by research. But his reputation has outlived such critics, for Cody the man deserves our attention: his legend is only a part of the story.

Cody himself, however, rarely reacted against his critics. If anything, he was his own worst enemy. His ability to tell a good yarn, even if it meant being economical with the truth, together with a poor memory for names and dates, confused even his own family. And it is here that his detractors have scored many cheap victories over him with little attempt at verification.

Probably the most damning allegations made against Cody are that he never rode for the Pony Express and never killed an Indian until he "shot" innumerable "supers" in his stage and "Wild West" career. It is true that historians have queried Cody's claim to have been a Pony Express rider. Some have accepted his published statements verbatim, or even embellished them still further; others have doubted virtually everything he wrote or said. The cause of all the doubt is Cody himself, for before the publication of his autobiography in 1879, there was no mention of Buffalo Bill as a Pony Express rider, and his revelation came as a surprise to many of those who had been involved in the epic venture.

Cody wrote that in 1859 he joined the Pike's Peak gold rush and that he and his companions constructed a raft to carry them west on the Platte River. At Julesburg it met with an accident and disintegrated, and they lost all of their possessions. George Chrisman, the station agent at Julesburg, then employed Cody as a Pony Express rider on a short route ("as I was so young") of forty-five miles. Cody worked the route for two months before returning home when he learned that his mother was unwell.

Later, Cody said that he joined Lew Simpson on a wagon train from Atchison, Kansas, to Fort Laramie and that William Russell, senior partner in the firm of Russell, Majors & Waddell, organizers of the Pony Express, gave him a letter to hand to Joseph A. ("Jack") Slade, the division superintendent and already one of the frontier's most notorious characters. When Cody presented Slade with the letter he was promptly hired as a Pony Express rider. At this point Cody launched into a lengthy description of his exploits, including an alleged ride of more than three hundred miles because his replacement had been killed in a drunken brawl. On another occasion, he wrote, the service was stopped when Indians drove off the company's stock. James B. Hickok (not yet known as "Wild Bill") was elected their captain, and he led a band of idle riders and stagecoach drivers on the trail of the Indians. The tracks led to their village on Clear Creek near Crazy Woman's Fork on the Powder River. During a night attack, they successfully stampeded and recovered their stock. Cody then wrote that he became a kind of "supernumerary rider" at Horseshoe Station, where he remained until 1861, when he returned to Leavenworth.[1]

Cody's confusion over dates is obvious. The Pony Express was not started until April 3, 1860, so he could not possibly have ridden for it as early as 1859, and his alleged adventures with Slade and Hickok are not borne out by the facts. In his close examination of Cody's narrative, Dr. John S. Gray established that the gold-seeking expedition took place in the summer of 1860, when Billy and his friend Arthur Patterson accompanied Cody's uncle Elijah and family on their move to Denver. Billy and Patterson were probably employed as teamsters for the trip. They returned to Leavenworth in November broke but wiser, and Billy Cody resumed his schooling. Based upon known evidence and some considerable research, Dr. Gray pinpointed the anomalies in Cody's story in a masterly manner and summed up the situation:

> Not just every book about Cody but every one about the Pony Express recites Cody's Pony Express exploits, even Alexander Majors' memoirs. All, however, are easily recognized as mere quotations, paraphrases, or embellishments of Bill's autobiography. There is but one tiny ember beneath these billows of smoke: for two months in the summer of 1857, the eleven-year-old Cody rode as messenger boy for Russell, Majors and Waddell within a three-mile radius of Leavenworth.

Dr. Gray, however, concluded that it "is unfortunate that Cody so clouded the truth with fiction, for the reality is an impressive record of character and fortitude."[2]

Additional research by Dr. Gray and others has also demolished Cody's claim that he killed an Indian in 1857 during a raid on a cattle herd he was helping to guard. But Cody's later career as an Indian fighter and scout is based upon much firmer evidence. His exploits with the Fifth Cavalry, when he killed Tall Bull and Yellow Hand (or Hair), are also better documented.

In 1872, Cody received the Medal of Honor for his courage in fighting Indians. It is generally believed that the medal was later withdrawn in 1913 when *Army Regulations* decreed that only enlisted men or officers were entitled to it, and his name was struck from the record. Correspondence in the National Archives, however, reveals that in 1916 the judge advocate general of the army and General H. P. McCain, the adjutant general, discussed Cody's right to the medal, and it was concluded that his heroics were "above and beyond the call of duty." His claim was approved. On November 29, 1916, Cody addressed a short but moving note to General McCain: "Yours of Nov. 9th with the Medal of Honor certificate recd. I thank you." Buffalo Bill's Medal of Honor is now on view at the Buffalo Bill Historical Center in Cody, Wyoming.

Any researcher who seeks the facts about Buffalo Bill can easily feel daunted by the sheer volume of material, much of it fictionalized. In this present study we have examined public and government records, and we have also consulted Don Russell's near-definitive work *The Lives and Legends of Buffalo Bill.* Similarly, Nellie Snyder Yost's intimate account of the family man, *Buffalo Bill: His Family,*

Friends, Failures, and Fortunes, has been most helpful. The late Mr. Russell's work was particularly useful in collating the first part of this book, which is a résumé of Cody's early life and scouting experiences brought up to date by more recent research. This, we hope, will establish Cody as a *bona fide* character before he was overshadowed by the showman, for it is as a showman that he is best remembered. Indeed, many of those brought up on the musical *Annie Get Your Gun* can be forgiven if they assume that Buffalo Bill was an old, white-haired peripheral character, while Annie was the star of the show. In reality, of course, it was Cody who was the star and its main attraction. And it says much for his character—and his ego—that when he forsook the frontier for the footlights in 1872, he was prepared to face ridicule in pursuit of fame and fortune.

The earliest known reference in print to William Frederick Cody as "Buffalo Bill" appeared in the *Leavenworth Daily Conservative* on November 26, 1867. Most Kansans, however, were more familiar with William ("Buffalo Bill") Mathewson, who arrived in the area in 1850 as an employee of the Northwestern Fur Company. In 1860, during a drought, he hunted buffalo to keep half-starved settlers and their families alive. They dubbed him "Buffalo Bill of the Plains." Rivalry between the two Buffalo Bills was later stirred up by press agents. Mathewson shrugged Cody off with this com ment: "The name of Buffalo Bill was tacked onto me before Bill Cody knew the difference between a buffalo and a jack rabbit." When the two men finally met at Wichita in 1911, Cody readily acknowledged that Mathewson had prior claim to the title, and the pair became friends.

Critics of Buffalo Bill have also included would-be temperance reformers, who have made frequent references to his alcoholic intake. We do not deny that he was sometimes high at noon and a friend to the distillery industry, but we do challenge some stories that suggest he was frequently drunk. Friends and contemporaries have confirmed that he liked his liquor, but none have ever accused him of being too drunk to perform. Rather, they praised his professionalism.

But it is Cody the man and not his legend that concerns us, for as his story unfolds we believe that the man will survive and surpass the myth. His love of life and inherent romanticism, especially toward the West of his youth and early manhood, led ultimately to the creation of the Wild West, and it is thanks to him that generations of youngsters (and the not so young) have enjoyed the romance and spectacle of a vanished era. Therefore, this pictorial biography is our tribute to a man who was so much more than a western myth.

Joseph G. Rosa and Robin May

London, England

NOTES

1 William F. Cody, *The Life of Hon. William F. Cody, Known as Buffalo Bill, The Famous Hunter, Scout and Guide: An Autobiography* (Hartford, Conn., 1879), 89–125.

2 John S. Gray, "Fact versus Fiction in the Kansas Boyhood of Buffalo Bill," *Kansas History* 8, no. 1 (Spring 1985): 19–20. Gray holds Ph.D. and M.D. degrees from Northwestern University, Evanston, Illinois, where he served on the medical school faculty until his retirement in 1974. His research into Old West characters has revealed much that was previously unknown. It was Dr. Gray who discovered that William Comstock was not part Indian, as many thought, and that he was related to James Fenimore Cooper.

ACKNOWLEDGMENTS

During the preparation of this book the authors enlisted the aid of a number of people, some by mail and others on a personal basis when they visited Cody, Wyoming; North Platte, Nebraska; and parts of Kansas. Therefore, initially, we should like to extend special thanks to Nellie Snyder Yost and the Friends of Buffalo Bill for arranging a visit to Scout's Rest Ranch and the opportunity to examine and obtain copies from the Rest's photographic collection; and Dr. Paul Fees, curator of the Buffalo Bill Historical Center, Cody, Wyoming, who provided us with prints from some of the center's thousands of photographs and allowed us access to the museum's collection of manuscript material. We are also indebted to the University of Nebraska Press, which kindly supplied Velox prints of the woodcuts from Cody's 1879 *Life*, which appeared in their own Bison edition published in 1978.

We should also like to thank (alphabetically) the following individuals and institutions for their assistance with both illustrations and other material: the late Tim Bannon; John Boessenecker; the Buffalo Bill Memorial Museum, Golden, Colorado; Emory Canty, Jr.; Colin Crocker; Paul and Penny Dalton; David Dary; Jack DeMattos; James D. Drees; Edith Harmon; Gregory Hermon; the late Ethel A. Hickok; Dr. Paul A. Hutton; Ida Ipe; Karl Kabelec, University of Rochester Library, Rochester, New York; Prof. James T. King; the late Dr. Richard Lane; the Leavenworth Public Library; George LeRoy; Dr. Hugh P. MacMillan, Archives of Ontario, Canada; the Mahoning Valley Historical Society; Greg Martin; the Nebraska State Historical Society; Thomas B. Morrison; the Kansas State Historical Society; Herb Peck, Jr.; Robert Pollock; the Royal Archives, Windsor Castle, for permission to quote from Her Majesty Queen Victoria's Journal; Melvin A. Schulte; William B. Secrest; Judge Arthur J. Stanley, Jr.; Lucile V. Stevens; Durrett Wagner; the Western History Department, Denver Public Library; Reed Whitaker, director, National Archives, Kansas City, Missouri, Branch; Bill Willson; R. Larry Wilson; and the Wyoming State Archives, Cheyenne.

1

THE MAKING OF
A PLAINSMAN

Buffalo Bill—the very name evokes an image of a tall, buckskin-clad figure astride a white horse, with vast rolling plains and mountains as a backdrop. His eyes are shielded from the blazing sun by a huge sombrero as, rifle in hand, he stares out across the prairie, ever watchful for Indian or buffalo—the personification of the western hero: an image that survives more than seventy years after his death.

William Frederick Cody, the man behind the legend, came originally from Iowa, where he was born at Leclaire, Scott County, on February 26, 1846, the second son of Isaac and Mary Cody.[1] The Codys could trace their origins back to one Philippe le Caude and his wife, Martha, who left the Island of Jersey and settled at Beverly, Massachusetts, in 1698. Isaac came from a Canadian branch of the family. He emigrated to the United States in 1838, where he met Mary Ann Laycock, who became his third wife in May 1840. Martha, Isaac's five-year-old daughter from a previous marriage, was accepted by Mary as her own, and the couple had seven more children. The eldest, Samuel, was born in 1841. He was followed by Julia in 1843, William Frederick in 1846, Eliza Alice in 1848, Laura Ella (Nellie or Helen to the family) in 1850, Mary Hanna in 1853, and Charles in 1855.[2]

When Samuel suffered a fatal fall from a horse in 1853, the grief-stricken family decided to move west, where the soon-to-

THIS photograph is alleged to be William Cody as a child of four. It has been published many times, but its authenticity has never been established. A carte-de-visite of this photograph owned by the Buffalo Bill Historical Center was examined recently, and it was doubted that the image is in fact William Cody. (Courtesy Kansas State Historical Society)

be-opened territory of Kansas beckoned. The Codys became one of the first families to settle in Kansas. They built a house at Salt Creek Valley some three miles west of Fort Leavenworth, which later became known as Kickapoo Town-

THE *Cody family's first Kansas home in Salt Creek Valley, some three miles west of* *Fort Leavenworth. (Courtesy Scout's Rest Ranch)*

ship. At first they were happy, but within months of their arrival the vexed question of slavery created problems. The government was well aware that the new territory would upset the balance of slave-owning and slave-free states, but rather than impose legislation one way or the other, it was decided that the territory's citizens themselves should decide if they wished to be a slave or a free state. This led to conflict between the pro- and anti-slavery factions, and Isaac was soon in trouble.

A lesser man would have kept his mouth shut, but Isaac, a God-fearing, staunch abolitionist in a largely proslavery community, could not hide his feelings. He joined the Salt Creek Squatters (or Claim) Association, and at a meeting held on September 18, 1854, he quarreled with an employee of his brother Elijah's, H. Charles Dunn, who stabbed him in the chest. The Liberty, Missouri, *Democratic Platform* of September 28 described Isaac as a "noisy abolitionist," and remarked that his wound was "not enough it is feared to cause his death. The settlers on Salt Creek regret that his

BILLY Cody and Prince ride to warn his father of a plot to kill him, as depicted in Cody's Life. Cody's riding skill and the fleetness of his pony enabled him to outdistance his pursuers.

THE stabbing of Isaac Cody by the nefarious H. Charles Dunn on September 18, 1854 (depicted in Cody's 1879 Life), made a lasting impression on the eight-year-old boy. His father's bouts of ill health and death three years later forced a maturity upon the boy beyond his years. ABOVE

THE death of Billy Cody's elder brother, Samuel, as depicted in Buffalo Bill's 1879 autobiography. LEFT

JAMES *Butler Hickok, ca. 1858, from a family tintype. The original is hand-tinted and is mounted in an ornate case. This print has been reversed to correct the mirror image. The young Hickok regarded Kansas as "no place for women and children yet." Of this portrait, believed made at Lawrence, he wrote: "I will send you my likeness and you can see whether it looks like a whisky face or not." (Courtesy the late Ethel Hickok)*

wound is not more dangerous, and all sustain Mr. Dunn in the course he took. Abolitionists will yet find 'Jordan a hard road to travel!'"

Isaac recovered, but he never again enjoyed good health. He died on April 21, 1857, from a severe chill. For young Billy Cody, his father's death was a terrible blow; he worshiped him and de-

clared him to be a martyr to the Kansas antislavery cause. Billy was now the man of the family. Mrs. Cody, however, insisted that between chores he and his sisters continue their education. She took in boarders, but that was not enough to sustain them, so she decided that Billy should get a job. One morning she appeared in Leavenworth at the offices of Russell, Majors & Waddell, where she persuaded Alexander Majors to give her son a job. The famous freight company had been formed in 1855 and was already the largest such organization on the plains. Billy was promptly put to work as a messenger riding between their office and the telegraph office at Fort Leavenworth some three miles away. He stayed two months with the company but thought that the job was "too confining for a country boy."[3]

In his autobiography, Cody wrote that he joined Lew Simpson's ill-fated wagon train, which was attacked by Mormons in October 1857. Here, he claimed, he first met James Butler Hickok, who interceded when Billy was bullied by a teamster. In fact neither Cody nor Hickok was with Simpson's train on that occasion. Billy was at home in Leavenworth, while Hickok was at Monticello in Johnson County. The Codys may well have met Hickok when he lived near Leavenworth for some months in 1856 (the following year he moved on to Monticello, and from there to Olathe); but it was 1859 before he became a regular visitor to the Cody home.[4]

BILLY Cody's assertion in later years, depicted in his Life, that he shot his "first Indian" in 1857 was, he claimed, written up in the Leavenworth Times. But no trace of the story has been found. We are forced to conclude that Buffalo Bill made up the yarn, perhaps crediting himself with a slaying that had been committed by someone else. LEFT

A SKETCH of Buffalo Bill's Tavern—the seven-room log house the family moved into in 1855. It later became a hotel, which Cody managed for a short time following his marriage in 1866. In the early years of this century, old-timers in Leavenworth recalled that long after Cody left the place it achieved a reputation as a "fast house," especially on a Saturday night. (Courtesy Leavenworth Public Library) RIGHT

BY the mid-1850s wagon trains bearing families or freight were a common sight on the plains. This woodcut from Cody's Life is an impressionistic sketch of a typical prairie schooner or freight wagon. Both oxen and Texas longhorn cattle were used to pull the lumbering wagons, and it took a number of "bullwhackers" to keep the beasts under control. ABOVE

When the Civil War broke out in 1861, Billy was among a number of young men who joined an ex–Free Stater named Chandler in some dangerous excursions into Missouri to steal horses from alleged ex–Border Ruffians. When his mother learned of his activities she was furious and ordered him to stop. It was fortunate that he did, for some months later, Chandler was killed when pursued by Union cavalry.

For the next two years Billy Cody's life was spent in and around Leavenworth doing odd jobs. In 1863 he joined a freight outfit en route to Denver. Here he learned that his mother was seriously ill and he hastened home. He arrived just before she died on November 22. "I loved her above all other persons," he wrote. In his grief he found solace in alcohol and gambling and mixed with "bad characters generally." A dramatic change came when the Seventh Kansas Cavalry Regiment returned to Leavenworth early in 1864. Under the command of Colonel C. R. Jennison, the regiment had achieved quite a reputation and was generally called "Jennison's Jayhawkers," the scourge of the Missouri Bushwhackers and ex–Border Ruffians. Billy decided to sign up, although he later claimed that his enlistment was the result of imbibing too much bad whiskey and he could not recall how or when he enlisted. But he was glad that he had, adding that "it would not do for me to endeavor to back out." According to the muster roll, Cody enlisted into Company F on February 19,

WILLIAM *Cody aged 12, ca. 1858, the year he made his first trip (with John Willis) across the plains as far as Fort Laramie. The photographer is not known, but at that time Leavenworth had several of them, including Short & Addis, who boasted "fine daguerreotypes." (Kansas Daily Herald, May 1, 1858). (Courtesy Kansas State Historical Society)*

1864. He was described as having brown eyes and brown hair and was then five feet ten inches in height.[5]

The Seventh Kansas fought in Tennessee before being pulled back to help in the defense of St. Louis and other campaigns. Cody later said he was employed as a spy and on one occasion met up with Wild Bill Hickok dressed as a Confeder-

MARY Ann Laycock Cody ca. 1860. This determined-looking but kindly lady took charge of her young family following her husband's death, and she worried over the welfare and future of her children, especially of William. When she died in 1863, Billy Cody was disconsolate. "I love her above all other persons," he wrote. It was her influence that guided his future course to success, fame, and fortune. (Courtesy Buffalo Bill Historical Center)

THIS contemporary painting of a Pony Express rider typifies the men and youths who rode "the pony" during the enterprise's eighteen months of glory. Cody claimed to have been a rider, but the facts do not support his assertion. Some recent research has also revealed that his mother was at odds with William H. Russell at this time. Mary Cody alleged that Russell and others (among them former U.S. Marshal Elias S. Dennis) had maltreated animals and removed stock and property following her husband's death. In court on April 7, 1860, the defendants were acquitted. This was only four days after the start of the Pony Express. The relationship between the Codys and Russell must have been at least somewhat strained (Case No. 412, Mary Cody vs. Elias S. Dennis, William H. Russell et al., U.S. District Court, Territory of Kansas, First Judicial District, Leavenworth Division, Federal Records Center, Kansas City, Mo.). (Courtesy Kansas State Historical Society)

BY 1864 James Butler Hickok was generally known in southwestern Missouri and parts of Arkansas as Wild Bill and served the Union as a scout and spy. This family tintype is thought to have been made at Springfield, Missouri, ca. 1864 and has been reversed to obtain the correct image. (Courtesy the late Ethel A. Hickok)

THIS photograph of Cody as a young private in the Seventh Kansas Cavalry was probably taken in 1864 or 1865. The original tintype is small enough to fit into a locket. The print has been reversed to obtain the correct image. (Courtesy Buffalo Bill Historical Center)

ate officer. Official records, however, reveal that he remained on the regimental roll as a private until his discharge on September 29, 1865.[6]

In the months immediately following the end of the Civil War on April 9, 1865, Cody was temporarily assigned to act as a hospital orderly at St. Louis. Here he met Louisa Frederici, the daughter of John Frederici, a native of Alsace-

Lorraine. Louisa recalled that she had first met Billy Cody on May 1, 1865, when he was a guest in her home. Soon Cody was a frequent visitor, and as a joke, the couple passed themselves off as engaged. He returned to Leavenworth where, he later asserted he found employment as a laborer and then as a stagecoach driver for Ben Holliday's Overland Stage Line. He then began receiving letters from Louisa reminding him of his promise of marriage. She accused him of not keeping his word, so he "concluded to do it," and they were married in St. Louis on March 6, 1866.

The marriage was a mistake, although at various times the pair tried to make a go of it. Louisa never accepted the West; neither did she appreciate Cody's later theatrical ventures. In fact, their periods of separation were far longer than the time they actually spent together. Nevertheless, Cody proved himself to be a good father to his children, and during the time when the marriage worked, both partners showed each other much affection. To Louisa he was always "Will," and to him she was always "Mama" or "Lulu."

The newlyweds settled into their home which was the same small residence-cum-hotel formerly owned by Cody's mother in Salt Creek Valley, now rented from Dr. J. J. Crook, former surgeon of the Seventh Kansas Regiment. Although Cody was determined to make a success of domesticity and hotel-keeping, he soon found it a dull life, and despite a promise to Louisa that he would not return to the plains, by September he had had enough. He relinquished his interest in the hotel and persuaded his wife to move in with his sister Helen at Leavenworth. He then left for the West. Louisa, however, soon tired of that arrangement and departed for St. Louis, by which time her husband was in and around Junction City, Kansas.

At Junction City, where the tracks of

the Union Pacific Railway Company (Eastern Division—U.P.E.D.) had just arrived and were extending west as far as Denver, Cody found Wild Bill Hickok, fresh from Santa Fe, where he had acted as a guide for General John S. Pope. Cody recalled that Hickok obtained employment for him as a scout and that during "the winter of 1866–67" he scouted between Fort Ellsworth and Fort Fletcher (renamed Fort Harker in 1867). Official records do not verify any such employment, but during that winter Cody was at the fort, where he shared a dugout on Mulberry Creek, Salina County, with a man named Henry A. Northrup. A part of that structure was still visible as late as 1925.[7]

In the summer of 1867, Cody visited the newly founded township of Ellsworth, near Fort Harker, where he met William Rose, a contractor for the U.P.E.D. Rose had a contract with Miller & Schoemaker for grading near Fort Hays. Cody joined him in this venture, and the pair also entered into a partnership to establish the township of New Rome, which was soon known as Rome, on the west bank of Big Creek. They chose the site in the belief that the railroad would pass that point (about a mile from Fort Hays), and they opened a store and a saloon there. Others joined them, and Louisa was even persuaded to come west and bring their daughter Arta, born on December 16, 1866.[8]

Rumors that Indians were about to attack the railroad led to frequent work

LOUISA *Maude Frederici from a tintype made at about the time of her marriage to Cody. Her large, dark, expressive eyes remained a dominant feature even in old age.*

This print has been reversed to obtain the correct image. (Courtesy Buffalo Bill Historical Center)

IN 1972 *the arms collection of the late William Goodwin Renwick was auctioned. Included was this pair of .41 caliber single-shot "derringer" pistols made by Henry Deringer of Philadelphia. Inscribed on the escutcheon plates of each pistol is*

W. F. Cody.
1865

According to papers in the Renwick Collec-tion at the Smithsonian Institution, Cody later presented the pistols to Louis A. Barker in appreciation of some personal service. Barker later gave them to Renwick. Cody probably purchased the pistols from a St. Louis, Missouri, gun dealer during his so-journ in the city in 1865. We doubt that he ever fired them in anger. The pistols are now owned by the Buffalo Bill Historical Center at Cody, Wyoming. (Courtesy Sotheby & Co.)

JUNCTION *City, Kansas, in 1867, pho-tographed by Alexander Gardner. The place looks peaceful enough, but its close proximity to Fort Riley made it a "garrison town," and the soldiers and civilians were often on a col-lision course. (Courtesy Kansas State His-torical Society)*

A CLOSE-UP *of the escutcheon inscription as it appears on both pistols. (Courtesy Sotheby & Co.)*

LOUISA'S *father, John Frederici, from a portrait made ca. 1875. (Courtesy Buffalo Bill Historical Center)*

ELLSWORTH, *Kansas, photographed by Alexander Gardner in 1867. The place was the haunt of freighters, buffalo hunters, scouts, and soldiers from nearby Fort*

Harker, and it achieved a statewide reputation for violence. (Courtesy Kansas State Historical Society)

FORT *Harker, Kansas, in September 1867. The garrison has turned out to be photographed by Alexander Gardner, who was photographing people and places on his tour for the Union Pacific Railway Company* (Eastern Division). Gardner's photographs *were later published in portfolio form or as stereoscopes. (Courtesy Kansas State Historical Society)*

stoppages. The workers often deserted their tasks and roamed the area. On August 5, the post commander at Fort Hays reported that "some Evil disposed person or persons" had informed the laborers that they had been ordered into the compound, as the fort was surrounded by hostile Indians. This news, and the added fear of cholera, which had broken out at Fort Harker, only added to their miseries. Later, on the twelfth, it was reported that individuals were selling "bad whiskey and intoxicating drinks" to the soldiers and civilians, which could prove "highly injurious to the health" of the post and was "in direct violation of the law of the

land." The army acted swiftly and confiscated large quantities of liquor on the grounds that the owners had no licenses. Among those who lost their "liquid assets" was one "W. F. Cody," who was relieved of four gallons of whiskey, three gallons of bitters, and other assorted liquors. Following the confiscation, there was a gradual return to work.[9]

Cody and Rose, meanwhile, were still convinced that the railroad would pass through Rome, and on August 20 a number of the town's citizens drew up a petition and applied to the state governor for the appointment of a justice of the peace. The request was refused on the grounds

THIS *woodcut from Cody's* Life *depicts the moment when he and his partner, Rose, ruefully contemplate the "fall of Rome," when its inhabitants finally quit following the railroad's switch to Hays City.*

that "Rome was not attached to Russell County for judicial purposes." When the U.P.E.D. finally reached Hays City in October, Rome was doomed.[10]

Cody's grading contract with Rose was getting them nowhere fast, and when for grading duties he finally had to hitch up his favorite horse, Brigham (named after the Mormon leader Brigham Young), he was very disillusioned. One morning, someone announced that a herd of buffalo had been sighted. The graders grew excited; they wanted fresh meat and Cody promptly offered to supply it. He unhitched Brigham, grabbed his rifle, and declared himself ready to ride. Few took him seriously, especially a group of cavalry officers who were themselves anxious to hunt the herd. Cody soon overtook them and within minutes had killed eleven buffalo. This so impressed the officers, particularly Captain George W. Graham of the Tenth Cavalry, that he offered Cody employment on similar hunts. It was not long before Graham and his fellow officers had dubbed Cody "Buffalo Bill."

A less romantic version of how Cody got the name appeared in the Hays City *Sentinel* of January 26, 1877, which stated that he "first made his appearance on the frontier as a mule whacker. In 1867–68

BUFFALO *Bill hunting with Captain Graham and men of the Tenth Cavalry, as depicted in his* Life.

he made his home in Hays and killed buffalo for a living; and his frequent appearance on our streets peddling meat gained for him the name of Buffalo Bill." The Goddard Brothers of Hays City, however, were quick to appreciate Cody's talents and contracted with him to supply meat for the workers. The contract called for twelve buffalo a day, for which he would be paid $500 a month. Cody was soon a familiar figure to the railroad gangs, and someone even coined a little jingle in his honor:

> Buffalo Bill, Buffalo Bill,
> Never missed and never will,
> Always aims and shoots to kill,
> And the company pays his buffalo bill.

Cody claimed later that over a period of eighteen months he killed 4,280 buffalo. Since his contract lasted less than eight months, his tally was probably closer to 3,000, for by May 1868 the end-of-track

crews had moved to what became Sheridan, Kansas.[11]

In between buffalo hunts Cody was also employed by the post quartermaster at Fort Hays as a "government detective," and he was provided with a letter authorizing him to obtain military assistance if required. When a number of men deserted from Fort Hays on March 5, 1868, and stole several government mules, Wild Bill Hickok was also alerted. Hickok made his home at Hays City where, in addition to building and running a saloon, he was employed as a deputy U.S. marshal. He and Cody joined forces; their pursuit of the deserters also led to the arrest of a number of known horsethieves. On the twenty-eighth Hickok requested that the post commander at Fort Hays provide a military escort to Topeka. Accompanied by six soldiers, he and Cody then transported the prisoners by rail and lodged them in jail. James Smith, the alleged leader of the gang of horsethieves, was later brought down in irons to face trial; but he was found not guilty when it was learned that one of the prisoners had perjured himself.[12]

When the U.P.E.D. reached a temporary halt at Sheridan, and his contract came to an end, Cody decided that he would seek permanent employment with the army. His worst moment came when he had to decide Brigham's fate. "Having no suitable place in which to leave my old and faithful buffalo-hunter Brigham, and not wishing to kill him by scouting,

SOUTH *Main Street, Hays City, ca. 1868. The transient population boasted a number of "bad men" and "desperadoes," but Cody managed to stay out of trouble and was never in a gunfight. (Courtesy Kansas State Historical Society)* TOP

FORT *Hays, Kansas, ca. 1869, when it was perhaps the most famous of the state's* Indian war posts. Cody was a familiar figure at the post; but we do not necessarily accept the claim made in the Hays City *Republican of July 28, 1894, that on one occasion Bill Howard, an assistant wagon boss at the fort, had kicked Buffalo Bill "all around the depot platform, and Cody had on two big Colt's revolvers, too." (Courtesy Kansas State Historical Society)* BOTTOM

I determined to dispose of him." After refusing several good offers, Cody finally raffled the animal. His new owner, Ike Bonham, took him to Wyandotte, Kansas, where he raced him. In 1876, during a visit to Memphis, Tennessee,

Cody learned that a former U.P.E.D. construction superintendent named Wilcox now owned the horse and was anxious that Cody should see him. Cody recalled that the reunion with Brigham was emotional. "It seemed as if he almost remembered me, and I put my arms around his neck, as though he had been a long-lost child."[13]

Cody's decision, in 1868, to seek employment with the army came at the height of Indian hostilities. There had been sporadic outbreaks right through the Civil War; but the spark that lit the powder keg came on November 29, 1864, when Colonel John M. Chivington and his Third Colorado Volunteers (aided and abetted by territorial governor John Evans) attacked a Cheyenne encampment at Sand Creek, Colorado Territory. The Indians believed themselves to be at peace with the United States and even flew the Stars and Stripes. Later, it was claimed that the camp was a reservation, which was incorrect. In fact, the band had gathered there in order to negotiate with Governor Evans. Apologists for Chivington alleged that because the Cheyenne tribe was at war with the whites, his actions were justifiable. Others demanded retribution, but he had already left the army before any action could be taken. The real significance of Sand Creek was that it led to a widespread war.

In 1865 the government signed a treaty with some of the plains tribes and persuaded them to move to Indian Territory (present-day Oklahoma). By 1867, however, hostile bands of Indians were again attacking settlements in Kansas. Major General Winfield Scott Hancock, in command of the Department of the Missouri, was then ordered to negotiate

with the tribes, and at the head of fifteen hundred men, he marched into Kansas.

"Hancock's Indian War" proved to be a dismal failure. Despite the presence of Delaware Indian scouts and some of the finest white scouts available, Hancock found few Indians. In October a Peace Commission met with the Indians at Medicine Lodge Creek, some seventy miles south of Fort Larned, where a semblance of peace was restored.

Cody claimed that he acted as a scout for General Custer in 1867, but it was 1868 before his name appeared in any official records. Scouting in an Indian war was extremely hazardous. Scouts, guides, and couriers risked their lives daily, carrying dispatches from one post to another or riding alone ahead of the troops in search of the enemy or of a safe route. Horses were generally used, but some thought that a good mule could make better time over rough country than could a horse. Armed with one or two revolvers, and perhaps a carbine, scouts and others traveled by night if possible, rather than by day. Courage alone was not enough; the venture required skill, cunning, a knowledge of the country, and a certain amount of luck to match a formidable foe. Yet there was no lack of volunteers.

By August 1868, both Cody and Hickok were employed by the Tenth Cavalry as scouts. Major George Armes noted in his journal for August 21 that his bitter enemy, Major M. H. Kidd (who was later relieved of his command and dis-

PLAINS *dwellers were ever on their guard against Indian attacks. This illustration is from a steel engraving on a Union military scrip for fifty dollars, issued in June 1867, as compensation for damages caused by Confederate General Sterling Price's raid in 1864. (From the collection of Joseph G. Rosa)*

charged from the army at his own request in 1870), had "failed to pay attention to the advice of Wild Bill our scout and guide, in regard to the course we should take when we left camp yesterday, he appearing to know more about the country than those who have lived here for years." Kidd found himself ten miles off course with no sign of Indians. On the twenty-fourth Armes recorded that "Bill Cody (Buffalo Bill) one of our scouts and one of the best shots on the plains, keeps us well supplied with plenty of Buffalo and deer. He gets $60 per month and a splendid mule to ride, and is one of the most contented and happy men I ever met."[14]

Later that same month Cody, who was attached as a scout to Fort Larned, volunteered to carry some important dispatches from Fort Larned to General Philip H. Sheridan at Fort Hays, some sixty-five miles away. At Fort Hays he learned that the same information was needed at Fort Dodge, a further ninety-five miles to the south. Sheridan called for a volunteer, and Cody stepped forward. Sheridan later recalled:

> Cody, learning of the strait I was in manfully came to the rescue, and proposed to make the trip to Dodge, though he had just finished his long and perilous ride from Larned. I gratefully accepted his offer, and after four or five hours' rest he mounted a fresh

horse and hastened on his journey. . . . At Dodge he took six hours' sleep and then continued to his own post—Fort Larned with more despatches. After resting twelve hours at Larned, he was again in the saddle with tidings for me at Fort Hays. . . . [Cody gave] such an exhibition of endurance and courage . . . enough to convince me that his services would be extremely valuable in the campaign, so I retained him at Fort Hays till the battalion of the Fifth Cavalry arrived, and then made him chief of scouts for the regiment.[15]

How much Sheridan was influenced by Cody's courage on this occasion boosted by his local reputation is difficult to assess, but his decision changed the course of Cody's life. His change of status came just at the right time, for the year 1868 was a crucial one in the Army's fight against hostile Indians, and many of the settlements prepared to be besieged.

Sheridan saw for himself the effects of the Indians' raids, and when General William Tecumseh Sherman ordered him to "compel" the warring tribes to return to their reservations, Sheridan took it upon himself to organize bands of volunteer militia. With only twenty-six hundred troops in the Department of the Upper Arkansas, eighteen hundred of whom were employed protecting forts, stagelines and railroads, he was left with only eight hundred troops to fight the Indians. Sherman was opposed to "militia"

COLONEL *George A. Armes attended a performance of Cody's Wild West in 1888. Cody was helpful when the colonel was purchasing some property. On December 31, 1893, Armes reported that he and Cody were aides to General Martin T. McMahon during President Cleveland's inauguration (Armes, Ups and Downs of an Army Officer, 580, 634). (Courtesy Kansas State Historical Society)*

organizations, but Sheridan had no choice; on August 24 he ordered Brevet Colonel George A. Forsyth, a major in the Ninth Cavalry regiment, to hire fifty first-class and hardy frontiersmen to be used as scouts. His second in command was Lieutenant Frederick Beecher. This band was attacked by a band of combined Sioux and Cheyenne led by the redoubt-

LIEUTENANT-*Colonel (Brevet Major General) George Armstrong Custer, whom Cody much admired. In his book* My Life on the Plains, *Custer made no mention of Cody. We suspect that Cody became acquainted with Custer in later years, particularly following the Grand Duke Alexis Buffalo Hunt in 1872. Buffalo Bill and Mrs. Custer exchanged several letters and reminiscences of the general. (Courtesy Herb Peck, Jr.)*

FORT LARNED, *Kansas, ca. November 1869. (Courtesy Kansas State Historical Society)*

able Roman Nose on September 17 on the Arickaree Fork of the Republican River. Beecher's band held out for nine days before relief arrived. Beecher was killed, and the place was named in his honor. The incident has become immortalized as "The Battle of Beecher Island."[16]

Cody did not have long to wait for the Fifth Cavalry. The regiment reached Fort Hays by rail on October 1 and by the fifth, under the command of Major Royall, they were on the march toward Prairie Dog Creek. Unknown to Cody, the post commander of Fort Larned had

written to Fort Hays pointing out that when he was transferred to Fort Hays he had by mistake been "furnished with a horse belonging to Co. A 10th Cavalry, which has not yet been returned." He requested that the animal be kept until arrangements could be made for its return. The Fifth, however, was well on its way "piloted by Bill Coady [sic], a noted scout who is well posted and as thoroughly initiated in the mysteries of the Indians as Satanta or Charley Bent. It is to be hoped he may be successful in leading the Fifth Cavalry into the very hearthstone of Mr. Lo."[17]

When the regiment was joined at Buffalo Tank by its new commander, Brevet Major General Eugene A. Carr, it was

GENERAL *Philip H. Sheridan, whose faith in Cody as a scout and a guide led to his appointment as chief of scouts of the Fifth Cavalry. The men maintained a lifelong friendship based on a mutual admiration for each other's accomplishments rather than for their social status. (Courtesy Kansas State Historical Society)*

GENERAL *Eugene Carr regarded Cody as one of the finest scouts on the plains. (Cour-* *tesy Kansas State Historical Society)*

FORT *Wallace, Kansas, ca. the early* *1870s. Cody's visits to the post were sporadic, but in 1868 and early 1869, he was* *at the place with Carr and the Fifth Cavalry. (Courtesy Kansas State Historical Society)*

Cody who awaited the arrival of his train. Carr recalled:

> While I was unloading my horses & Baggage I saw a man in buckskin with a broad hat sitting on a horse on some rising ground not far from the station. Thinks I "There is one of those confounded scouts posing." Some of them mostly fakes are apt to hang around railroad stations & tell big stories to tenderfeet. Pretty soon he rode down to me & said Col Royall's command was camped on the Saline about 3 miles off, & if I wished he would ride down & tell him and he would send an ambulance for me. I said "you may if you want to."[18]

That meeting led to a long association and a lifelong friendship between Cody and the general. Carr recalled Buffalo Bill as a "wonderful shot" who "killed antelope running" and who had "eyes as good as a fine field glass, and was the best white trailer I ever saw. One of his qualities was a trained knowledge of the country . . . and he could pick the best route for a wagon train. He rode down a good many horses[;] but it paid to furnish them as it saved the rest."[19]

At Fort Wallace, Carr found Sheridan awaiting him. Sheridan was anxious that Carr prepare himself for the next phase of the planned winter campaign. Sheridan's plan was relatively simple: he would strike at the Indians in their winter retreats in a three-pronged attack from three principal forts. One column would come from Fort Bascom, New Mexico, under the command of Captain A. W. Evans, and from Forts Lyon and Dodge, Carr and Captain William H. Penrose of the Third Infantry would lead the other columns. Overall strategy would be in the hands of Sheridan and Custer from a base camp at Camp Supply, I. T. (Indian Territory).

On November 27 Custer attacked Black Kettle's Cheyenne village on the Washita, killing an estimated 103 Indians, including women and children, and capturing the pony herd. About 53 women and children were also taken. Penrose, Carr, and Evans, meanwhile, were active in the field, but they were considered "beaters"—flushing out Indians—rather than attacking forces.

Penrose's command left Fort Lyon on November 11 and consisted of about 250 men led by about 18 scouts and guides. Among them was the celebrated Autobees family, Charles and his sons Mariano and Jesse. There were also Jesse Nelson and Wild Bill Hickok. By December the command had gotten lost and snowed in on the Paolo Duro, where Carr's command found them on the twenty-first. The men were starving, and many of the animals were dead. The situation was not helped when Cody and Hickok hijacked a beer train, an event that led to a drunken brawl, during which Hickok soundly thrashed Mariano Autobees.

General Carr saw to it that Cody and Hickok were actively employed elsewhere. By February, the troops had struggled back to Fort Lyon, depressed by the knowledge that they had accomplished almost nothing, although Carr in his official report hoped that they "had done something towards the success of the general plan of campaign." They had all endured great hardship but had shown themselves to be soldiers.[20]

Wild Bill Hickok allowed his enlistment as a scout to expire on February 28, 1869. He then returned to Kansas. Cody, however, decided that he would stay with the Fifth Cavalry. When the command reached Fort Lyon, most of the scouts and guides had been paid off, but Carr told Cody he did not wish to lose him. Cody found to his joy that he had received a pay raise backdated to the previous October. He now earned $125 per month. But Cody was exhausted, and Carr readily agreed to his request for leave to visit his family in St. Louis. Cody left his horse and a mule with Dave Perry at Sheridan and took the train to St. Louis. On his return, however, he learned that a government clerk, for reasons best known to himself, had informed the army that Cody had sold government property to Perry. The animals had been confiscated by the army and taken to Fort Wallace. Cody was furious. Despite Cody's explanation, Colonel Bankhead, post commander at Fort Wallace, called Cody a liar and refused to discuss the

FORT McPherson photographed in the late
1860s or early 1870s. (Courtesy Nebraska
State Historical Society)

matter. Cody promptly sought out the
clerk and soundly thrashed him, and the
clerk complained to Bankhead. Cody was
arrested and placed in the post guard-
house. When he tried to send a telegram
seeking assistance from General Sheridan, Bankhead ordered the message
stopped. Cody advised the colonel that
he had no legal right to stop a public
message. Finally, having extracted a
promise from Cody that he would not
molest the hapless clerk any further,
Bankhead returned Cody's animals to
Cody. On his return to Fort Lyon, where
Cody told his story to Carr and others,
who thoroughly enjoyed it, he found that
his services as a "government detective"
were again in demand.[21]

Two men, William ("Bill") Bevins and
a man named Williams, stole several
mules from the post. Cody was ordered to
pursue, and he was accompanied by
William Hamilton ("Bill") Green, Jack
Farley, and a man identified only as
"Long Doc." The thieves were tracked to
Denver, where they were arrested.
Williams managed to escape, and when
Bevins was handed over to the civilian
authorities, he was released. Later, fol-
lowing a career as a horsethief in the
Black Hills, Bevins was captured and
jailed.[22]

In May 1869, the Fifth Cavalry was ordered to Fort McPherson, and the post
became Cody's home until December
1872. By now Buffalo Bill was renowned
as a scout and guide. Carr regarded him
highly and on one occasion managed to
persuade the government to grant Cody
"one hundred dollars extra for extraor-
dinarily good services as a trailer and

BUFFALO *Bill dedicated this photograph to his "old scouting Pard, Jack Farley" at about the turn of the century. The existence of Mr. Farley has been queried many times, but this photograph and other evidence has proved that he was indeed one of Cody's "pards."* (Courtesy William B. Secrest) LEFT

fighter in my late pursuit of hostile Indians."[23]

It was at Fort McPherson that Cody first met Major Frank North, commander of the famous Pawnee battalion of Indian scouts, and his brother Luther. Cody recalled that he and Frank became great friends, but his relationship with Luther was cool.

Carr appreciated the Pawnees, but said that he had "always been opposed to the enlistment of Indians and negroes." Nevertheless, he remained loyal to government policy, realizing that scouts and trailers were necessary and the best should be employed regardless of race, for there were "very few 'Buffalo Bills'" to choose from.[24]

When Tall Bull and his Cheyenne "Dog Soldiers," a military organization or society within the tribe, went on the warpath and killed or kidnapped whites, Carr was ordered to pursue them. On July 11 during a fight, which was later celebrated as the "Battle of Summit Springs," Tall Bull was shot from the saddle and killed. Cody received credit for his death, but Luther North always maintained that it was his brother Frank and not Cody who had fired the fatal shot. For his part,

MAJOR *Frank North, from a family tintype. His brother Luther claimed that he was one of the best pistol shots on the plains, but he is best remembered for his exploits as the commander of the famous Pawnee Scouts. In the mid-1870s he and Cody became partners in a ranch on the South Fork of the Dismal River, sixty-five miles from North Platte. It was later sold, in 1882, to the John Bratt Company for $75,000. In 1883, Frank joined Buffalo Bill's Wild West. At Hartford, Connecticut, in 1884, he was severely injured when his saddle turned, and he was thrown under the hooves of a number of horses. He returned to Nebraska, where he died, mourned by the whole cast of the Wild West and in particular by the Pawnees, who regarded him as a father figure (Donald F. Danker, ed., Man of the Plains, 279n, 282).* (Courtesy Nebraska State Historical Society)

EDWARD *Zane Carroll Judson, alias Ned*   *(Courtesy Emory Canty, Jr.)*
Buntline, who persuaded Cody to go on stage.

LUTHER *North ca. 1867. (Courtesy Nebraska State Historical Society)*

Cody was more interested in the Indian's horse, which he swiftly captured and named Tall Bull. He recalled later that it was "the fastest runner in the state of Nebraska."[25]

In July 1869, Buffalo Bill met Edward Zane Carroll Judson, alias Ned Buntline, the prolific author of numerous "blood and thunder" novels. At that time Ned was supplementing his writings by a series of temperance lectures. He was due to appear at Fort McPherson and later at Fort Sedgwick. It was agreed that he could accompany a detachment of the Fifth Cavalry en route from McPherson to Fort Sedgwick. He spent most of the journey talking with Buffalo Bill. Cody probably took little interest in his many questions, but in December when Buntline's *Buffalo Bill, King of the Border Men* was published, Cody became a western hero overnight.

In 1870 Cody met John B. Omohundro, alias "Texas Jack," who arrived at Fort McPherson where he was soon employed as a scout and guide. In 1872 Jack was appointed trail agent for the Pawnees. The two became great friends, little suspecting the fame that they would achieve within a couple of years.

Buffalo Bill's expertise as a buffalo hunter proved beneficial both to his career and to his pocket. In September 1871, General Sheridan organized a hunt for a number of his New York friends. Many historians think this hunt presaged Cody's eventual decision to form the Wild West exhibition. Led by General Sheridan and with Cody as their guide, the party left Fort McPherson en route to Fort Hays, Kansas. For ten days they hunted buffalo, antelope, and other varieties of wildlife. Although Cody's reputation as an Indian fighter and plainsman had convinced many of the party that they would be confronted by a "desperado," they were agreeably surprised to find that

> Buffalo Bill . . . was a mild, agreeable, well-mannered man, quiet and retiring in his disposition, though well informed and always ready to talk well and earnestly upon any subject of in-

MOSES *Embree Milner, alias "California Joe," from a tintype believed to have been made at Pioche City, Nevada, ca. 1873. Born in Kentucky in 1829, Milner went West at an early age and by the mid-1860s had acquired his nickname and a reputation as a scout and guide. Custer promoted him to chief of scouts prior to the Washita campaign, but Joe got drunk and was demoted. He and Custer remained friends. Joe numbered Cody and Hickok among his many friends. He was a familiar sight at various army posts. He was murdered at Fort Robinson, Nebraska, on October 29, 1876, by Tom Newcomb, who shot him in the back. Newcomb escaped justice but not the hatred of Joe's many friends, who forced him to flee the country. (From the collection of Joseph G. Rosa)* RIGHT

THIS *photograph of Texas Jack Omohundro was taken by Varley of Baltimore, Maryland, ca. 1877, and is signed on the back in pencil "J. B. Omohundro, Texas Jack." (From the collection of Joseph G. Rosa)*

terest, and in all respects, the reverse of the person we had expected to meet. Tall and somewhat slight in figure, though possessed of great strength and iron endurance; straight and erect as an arrow, and with strikingly handsome features, he at once attracted to him all with whom he became acquainted, and the better knowledge we gained of him during the days he spent with our party increased the good impression he made upon his introduction.[26]

When he led the party out from Fort McPherson, Cody rode a "snowy white horse," and was dressed in a "suit of light buckskin, trimmed along the seams with fringes of the same leather, his costume lighted by the crimson shirt worn under his open coat, a broad sombrero on his head, and carrying his rifle lightly in his hand, as his horse came toward us on an easy gallop, he realized to perfection the bold hunter and gallant sportsman of the prairies."

THIS *romanticized view of Cody as a buffalo hunter was published in his 1879* Life.
*By his own statement, he shot the animals
while on the run and not as portrayed in the
illustration.* ABOVE

WILLIAM *Averill Comstock, the celebrated Medicine Bill, chief scout at Fort Wallace, regarded as one of the best scouts on the
plains. This photograph is thought to have
been made by Charles T. Smith of Topeka
ca. 1867. (Courtesy Kansas State Historical
Society)* RIGHT

For once Cody was not riding his favorite horse, Buckskin Joe, an animal he had first seen ridden by one of the Pawnees prior to the fight with Tall Bull. He had managed to persuade the Indian to part with it, but because it was an army horse he could not purchase it. Later, however, when the animal was condemned as unfit for army use, Cody bought it and kept it on his ranch at North Platte until its death, by which time it was stone blind. On this occasion, though, the honor of riding Buckskin Joe went to Leonard W. Jerome, whose second daughter Jennie later married Lord Randolph Churchill in 1874 and was the mother of Winston Churchill. Buckskin Joe disgraced himself by chasing after a buffalo on his own when his illustrious rider dismounted in order to take a careful shot at the "critter."

Cody's expertise, common sense, and homespun philosophy endeared him to his companions who named one of the overnight stops "Camp Cody, after our guide, philosopher and friend, Buffalo Bill." When the party entrained at Hays City for New York, Henry E. Davies, one of the party and the author of a book on the subject, declared, "We shook hands and exchanged a hearty good-bye with Buffalo Bill, to whose skill as a hunter, and experience as a guide, we were so much indebted."[27]

Buffalo Bill's exploits as a buffalo hunter inspired many myths, one, apparently, promoted by himself. He claimed in 1879 that he and the celebrated scout William ("Medicine Bill") Comstock competed for the title of "Champion Buffalo Killer of the Plains." No firm date was given, but it was thought to be 1868. Cody wrote that the contest was arranged by officers at Fort Wallace who backed Comstock. "It was accordingly arranged that I should shoot him a buffalo-killing match, and the preliminaries were easily and satisfactorily agreed upon. We were to hunt one day of eight hours beginning at eight o'clock in the morning, and closing at four o'clock in the afternoon. The wager was five hundred dollars a side, and the man who should kill the greater number of buffaloes from one horseback was to be declared the winner."

The hunt took place twenty miles east of Sheridan, and as it had "been pretty well advertised and noised abroad, a large crowd witnessed the interesting and exciting scene. An excursion party, mostly from St. Louis, consisting of about a hundred gentlemen and ladies, came out on a special train to view the sport, and among the number was my wife, with little baby Arta, who had come to remain with me for a while."

Both contestants agreed to go into the same herd and "make a run." Cody was convinced that he had both the best horse and the best gun, his famous "Lucretia Borgia," a .50 caliber Springfield rifle converted from its original percussion to the Allin breech-loading system. Fitted with a long firing pin, it was mis-

BUFFALO Bill ca. 1867–1870, from a rare tintype owned by the Garlow family. This is an important photograph, for it depicts Cody armed with his favorite buffalo rifle, the legendary "Lucretia Borgia." The barrel, action, and a part of the stock are now at the Buffalo Bill Historical Center. The other scout and the two army officers have not been identified. (Courtesy Buffalo Bill Historical Center)

takenly called a "needle gun" by Cody and other plainsmen. Comstock, however, was armed with a .44 rimfire sixteen-shot Henry repeating rifle. At the end of the day-long hunt (with a break for a champagne lunch), Cody, who had ridden Brigham part of the time without bridle or saddle, had killed sixty-nine buffalo to Comstock's forty-six, and "thereupon the referee declared me the winner of the match, as well as the champion buffalo-hunter of the plains."[28]

In her fictionalized memoirs, Louisa Cody reproduced the text of the "glaring poster," which, she claimed, flaunted "forth from a wall" of a building in St. Louis advertising the proposed event:

GRAND EXCURSION
to
FORT SHERIDAN

KANSAS PACIFIC RAILROAD

Buffalo Shooting Match
for
$500 a side
and the
Championship of the World
between

Billy Comstock (the famous scout)
and
W. F. Cody (Buffalo Bill)

FAMOUS BUFFALO KILLER
FOR THE KANSAS PACIFIC RAILROAD

This text contains several errors: The Union Pacific Railway Company (Eastern

Wild Bill's First Trail.

For Sale by "The New York News Co."
8 SPRUCE STREET.
(Opposite Tribune Buildings,) New York.

BUFFALO *Bill's rise to fame via the* New York Weekly *was presaged by his friend Hickok's appearance in DeWitt's Ten Cent* Romances, *issues nos. 3 and 10, published in 1867.* Wild Bill, the Indian Slayer, *and* Wild Bill's First Trail *enthralled a wide audience. Illustrated is the cover of issue no. 10. (Courtesy Library of Congress)*

Division) did not become the Kansas Pacific *Railway* until March 1869. "Fort Sheridan," founded in 1886 and named after the general, was twenty-four miles north of Chicago, whereas Sheridan, Kansas (also named after the general), was about twelve miles northeast of Fort

Wallace. We suspect that Louisa's coauthor invented the text of the poster. It is unlikely that Comstock would have involved himself in such a publicity-seeking venture, for he was wanted for murder at the time. In January 1868, at Fort Wallace, he had shot down an unarmed man named Wyatt, who he claimed owed him $2,200 but who refused to pay. Evidently provoked by Wyatt's boast that he had once ridden with Quantrill, Comstock had acted totally out of character. Comstock was removed to Fort Hays where, following a preliminary hearing, he was discharged for want of evidence. A warrant for his arrest was later issued but was never served. In August, while on a mission for General Sheridan, he was killed by Indians near Big Sandy Station. His remains were later brought to Fort Wallace for burial.[29]

The question remains, Did Cody make up the story of the buffalo-hunting match, or did such an event take place, but with participants unknown on the plains? This latter theory is prompted by a comment by the editor of the Boston *Transcript* of December 15, 1869, who published the first episode of Buntline's *Buffalo Bill, King of the Border Men* (which was then taken over by the *New York Weekly*). He wrote: "Buffalo Bill . . . is the *nom de chasse* of Wm. F. Cody, the greatest hunter, guide and scout in the far West. . . . A man who has killed sixty-nine buffaloes in one day's hunt."[30]

Others, including Lord Dunraven, enlisted Cody's services as a hunter and guide, but it was the hunt arranged for the Grand Duke Alexis of Russia that is best remembered and most publicized. During the summer of 1871, Alexis, the third son of Czar Alexander I, having expressed the desire to do so on several occasions, paid an official visit to the United States. The czar had approached President Grant with the request that the prince be allowed to visit the United States, in particular the western region. Grant readily agreed. Relations between the nations were good, for it had been barely four years since William H. Seward had negotiated the purchase of Alaska from the Russians, and Russia had actively supported the Union's cause during the Civil War. General Sheridan was then given the task of organizing the trip. The prince had expressed a desire to hunt, so Sheridan decided to arrange something special for him.

Escorted by a Russian battle fleet, the grand duke sailed from Falmouth, England, in September 1871. He received a warm welcome in the United States. Following a visit to the Smith & Wesson factory at Springfield, Massachusetts, where he was presented with a fine pistol, he paid a brief visit to Canada before heading for St. Louis, which he reached on or about New Year's Day 1872. His entourage then went by train to North Platte, Nebraska.

The Fifth Cavalry had been ordered to Arizona Territory on November 27, 1871, but on Sheridan's order Cody was left behind. Some weeks later the Third Cavalry

THE *original of this photograph of Buffalo Bill's cabin at Fort McPherson is a* carte-de-visite *ca. 1870. It was the Cody family's first home in the area and their residence dur-* *ing the period in which Buffalo Bill scouted for the troops at the post. (Courtesy Buffalo Bill Historical Center)*

arrived to garrison the post. Cody learned of his own part in the royal hunt.

By early January 1872 preparations for the grand duke's visit were well under way. A large buffalo hunt was to be the main event, and Spotted Tail and about a thousand Indians were persuaded to take part. Besides Spotted Tail there were such notables as War Bonnet, Black Hat, and Whistler, all formidable warriors. Whistler's presence, however, caused some concern, for he was known to have waged war against the whites only a short time before the hunt, and his subsequent murder by white men in the fall almost caused a war.[31]

The grand duke reached North Platte on January 13 and was accompanied by everything necessary for such a hunt, to-gether with one thousand barrels of to-bacco for the Indians, to whom only gold and whiskey were more prized. The London *Times's* correspondent, in a report dated January 17 and published on the thirty-first, penned what must surely be one of the first mentions of Cody in the British press: "'Buffalo Bill,' a famous hunter of that animal, met the Grand Duke at the railway station, and reported buffalo to be plenty within ten miles of the camp." An undated clipping stated that when General Sheridan, accompanied by Alexis, stepped down from the train and approached Cody, he said simply: "Your Highness, this is Mr. Cody, otherwise and universally known as Buffalo Bill. Bill, this is the Grand Duke." Cody replied, "I am glad to know you."[32]

FOLLOWING *the Grand Buffalo Hunt, Duke Alexis and his entourage, accompanied by notable army officers, appeared in Topeka, where this formal photograph was made. General Sheridan is seated on the* *duke's right. To his left and with his coat draped across his shoulders sits General Custer. (Courtesy Kansas State Historical Society)*

Cody recalled the duke as a "large, fine-looking young man," but got little opportunity to speak to him, for he was soon surrounded by other celebrities such as General Custer, General Ord, and General Forsyth (of Beecher Island fame), all of whom were enthralled by the prospect of such a huge hunt. Later, however, the grand duke questioned Cody closely concerning his choice of weapons, horse, and other necessities. Buffalo Bill assured him that he would have the best horse available (Buckskin Joe), and he would be instructed on which weapon to use. The first hunt took place at nine o'clock the following morning, and the duke chose a revolver as his weapon. No one, of course, questioned his decision. "He fired six shots from this weapon at buffaloes only twenty feet away from him, but as he shot wildly, not one of his bullets took effect," Cody recalled. He immediately exchanged pistols with him, but the result was the same. Anxious that Alexis should not feel humiliated, Cody gave him his trusted rifle, "Lucretia Borgia," and told him to get close to the buffalo. At the same time he slapped Buckskin Joe's rump so that the animal bounded closer to the big bull. "Now is your time," Cody yelled, and the duke fired, bringing down the buffalo. He immediately jumped down from his horse, threw his rifle to the ground, and waved his hat. Cody could not understand a word he uttered, but the champagne was soon uncorked in honor of the duke's first buffalo—the first of the hunt.[33]

The remainder of the hunt passed with spectacular performances by the Indians, whose hunting techniques with the bow and arrow impressed everyone. Even Alexis had one further moment of glory; he fired his revolver at a buffalo thirty feet away and the buffalo stumbled and fell. And at the close of the hunt, at Sheridan's request, Cody treated the prince to a hair-raising ride in an open carriage at breakneck speed to the railroad station. The ride left Alexis breathless with excitement. Announcing that he had thoroughly enjoyed himself, Alexis showered presents on everybody. To Buffalo Bill he presented a Russian fur coat, a diamond stick pin, and jeweled cufflinks and studs, all of which, apart from the cufflinks, have since disappeared. But for Cody the hunt had presaged something that would soon dominate his whole life. This first Wild West exhibition had proved an unqualified success, his name and fame were now nationwide, and people in power were interested in him.

Generals Sheridan and Ord suggested to Cody that he seek a commission in the army, but he declined, for he earned almost as much per month as a lieutenant and, besides, he had freedom of movement when his duties were completed. He did, however, accept an invitation by James Gordon Bennett and others to visit New York. Leaving his wife and children at Fort McPherson, Cody obtained a leave of absence until the end of March, and early in February he set out for the East. En route he met Professor Henry A. Ward, who had been a member of a hunting party several years before. Ward showed him the sights of Niagara Falls, and Cody then went on to New York. Here he was lionized by his erstwhile hunting companions. His long hair and habit of wearing a sombrero even with evening dress attracted much attention, but Cody soon overcame his initial shyness. He again met Ned Buntline. The meeting led to some friction with his hosts, who did not approve of Buntline. Buntline managed to get Cody to visit the Bowery Theater where Fred G. Maeder's melodrama based on *Buffalo Bill, King of the Border Men* was playing to packed houses. J. B. Studley was "Buffalo Bill," and when Buntline let the audience know that the original was among them, they roared their approval. He was persuaded to go on stage and take a bow but soon beat a hasty retreat. "I never felt more relieved in my life," Cody recalled, "than when I got out of the view of that immense crowd."[34]

Buntline offered Cody $500 per week

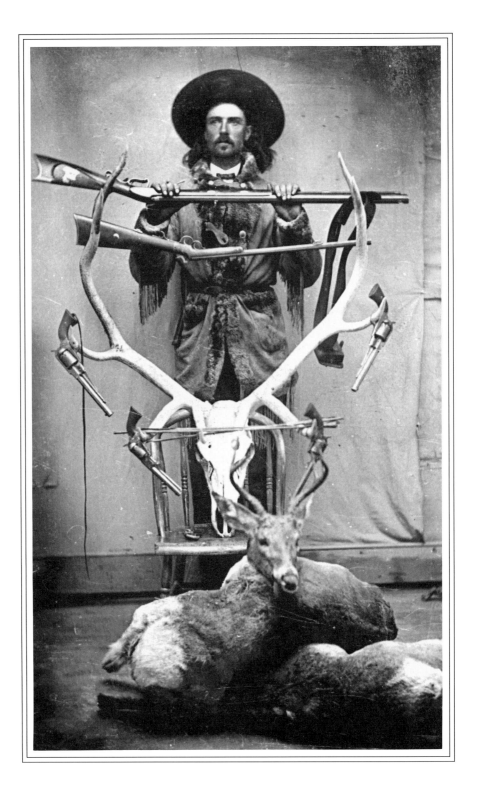

THIS "unknown" hunter, surrounded by an arsenal of weapons and dead animals, is believed to be from ca. 1871. Strong magnification, and a comparison of the costume worn by Cody in several of his photographs, has convinced us that this tintype is of Buffalo Bill and was probably made at Fort McPherson. (Courtesy Herb Peck, Jr.)

to play himself, but Cody declined and continued his tour. Back at Fort McPherson he resumed his duties as a scout. In one memorable engagement, during which he and some troopers were attacked by about eleven angry Indians anxious to avenge companions killed (one of them by Cody) in an earlier skirmish, they successfully held them off until the remainder of the command appeared. Cody then gave chase to about six Indians who abandoned some stolen horses and eventually escaped. In commending his conduct, Charles Meinhold added: "Mr. William Cody's reputation for bravery and skill as a guide is so well established that I need not say anything else but that he acted in his usual manner." As a result of his actions, Cody was awarded the Medal of Honor on May 22, 1872.[35]

In between his scouting and other duties, Cody continued to guide hunting parties and in the fall was put up as a Democratic candidate for the Nebraska legislature from the twenty-sixth district, a predominantly Republican area. He was elected by forty-four votes. "That is the way in which I acquired my title of Honorable," he wrote later. However, when he failed to claim his seat, it was contested by his opponent. Following an extraordinary mix-up over votes and procedure, D. F. Ashburn gained the seat by a majority of forty-two. After a brief experience as a justice of the peace, Cody's political life was over.[36]

During the summer of 1872, Buntline began bombarding Cody and Texas Jack with letters urging them with the promise of plenty of money to go East and engage in theatricals. Much soul searching and a review of his future prospects as a scout convinced Cody that he should give it a try, and on November 30, he and Texas Jack were paid off as scouts. Louisa's reaction, according to her memoirs, was favorable. She quotes Cody as saying that "I don't know just how bad I'd be at actin'. I guess maybe I'd better find out." Jack, however, was over the moon, for he was determined to be an actor "whether the audience said he could act or not." After their house was sold, Louisa and the children went to her parents' home in St. Louis, while Cody and Texas Jack headed for Chicago, where they were met by Buntline on December 12.[37]

Buntline was delighted to see them but miffed that they had arrived alone, not accompanied by ten Sioux and Pawnee chiefs, as Buntline had advertised that day in the Chicago *Evening Journal*. He told them that the Indians were essential to the play. He soon cheered up, however, when he realized that it was Buffalo Bill's presence that was most important.

For Cody and the slightly bemused Texas Jack, the sudden break from the frontier was traumatic. It was also a shock to learn that Buntline had not even auditioned for the play—let alone written it! Within hours, however, he had drafted the melodrama *Scouts of the Prairie* and hired James Nixon's Amphitheater for $1,000 for one week. Buntline committed the pair to learning their parts for a rehearsal the following morning. Both scouts thought that they could never remember a line; when Buntline cautioned them against reciting cues, Cody retorted: "Cues be d——d, I never heard of anything but a billiard cue!"[38]

The press, meanwhile, enjoyed speculating over the appearance or nonappearance of Sioux and Pawnee braves said to be straight from the plains, greased, painted, and dangling fresh scalps from their belts. It was then learned that the Indians were engaged in a "horse-stealing expedition, and in their places there have been substituted a selection of talented supers in tan-colored frocks and cambric pantalettes."[39]

Scouts of the Prairie played to a packed house on December 17. It was claimed that more than two thousand boys and young men crowded into the theater, and the "presence of 2,200 bad breaths and twice as many unclean feet" encouraged the scouts to do their best. The critics roasted the performance but praised the efforts of Guiseppina Morlacchi, premiere danseuse, who was later to marry Texas Jack. Yet even their severest critics could

BUFFALO *Bill and Professor Henry A. Ward ca. 1871, from a photograph by Stacy of Brooklyn. A companion plate depicts Cody looking more serious and the professor grasping a carbine. The two shared a friendship and correspondence that covered several years. Texas Jack Omohundro also corresponded with Ward and on one occasion sent him an inscribed photograph of himself. (From the collection of Joseph G. Rosa)*

not ignore the fact that the *real* Buffalo Bill and the *real* Texas Jack eclipsed any criticism there might be of their actual performances.[40]

Cody's recollections of that first night consisted of a mixture of powder-smoke (when dispatching forty or fifty extras dressed as Indians), rough-and-tumble fights, and tall tales around a fake campfire. Some critics later expressed the view that as an actor Cody was ridiculous, whereas Texas Jack was "not quite so good looking, not so tall, and not so straight, and not so ridiculous."[41]

By the time the first season ended at Port Jervis, New York, on June 16, 1873, the company's receipts were excellent. Cody, however, was not satisfied with the $6,000 he received. He thought that he should have received more. Texas Jack's reaction is unrecorded, but his biographer intimates that like Cody, he thought that Buntline had taken advantage of them. Buntline refused to budge, so he and the scouts split up. Cody was tempted to return to the West, but Omohundro persuaded him to remain on stage. First,

BUFFALO *Bill ca. 1873–74, dressed in the same beaver-trimmed coat he is wearing in the group photograph with Green, Hickok, Omohundro, and Overton (see p. 54). Thrust into his belt is what appears to be a .44 caliber Remington New Model Army percussion revolver of 1863. The Remington rolling-block rifle, which appears in several poses, was later presented by Cody to his friend Moses Kerngood and now belongs to the Buffalo Bill Historical Center. (Courtesy Buffalo Bill Historical Center)*

however, they needed a rest. They decided to head westward for the summer and hunt game.

At St. Louis Cody was reunited with his wife and family, who were to accompany him to Fort McPherson. Interviewed by the local press prior to his departure for Nebraska, Cody remarked that

we have played New York until we forced Edwin Booth to go West. He said it would not do for him to try to buck against us, and he was right. I propose to [be] . . . playing Shakespeare right through, from beginning to end, with Ned Buntline and Texas Jack to support me. I shall do Hamlet in a buckskin suit and when my father's ghost appears "doomed for a certain time," &c., I shall say to Jack, "Rope the cuss in, Jack!!" and unless the lassoo breaks, the ghost will have to come. As Richard the Third I shall fight with pistols and hunting knives.

In "Romeo and Juliet" I will put a half-breed squaw on the balcony, and make various interpretations of Shakespeare's words to suit myself.

Fortunately for posterity and the prose of the "immortal bard," Cody restricted his ambitions to blood-and-thunder border dramas. It was left to future generations to interpret Shakespeare.[42]

On his return from a hunt with several New York celebrities, Cody was interviewed by the *Omaha Daily Bee,* which published some of his comments on July 28, 1873. Cody proposed to produce a new play for the 1873–74 season, tentatively entitled *Buffalo Bill and Alexis on the Plains.* The drama would include horses and daring feats of equestrianism. He announced that he intended to tour Europe and would be "accompanied by James B. Hickok, the original 'Wild Bill.'" Cody anticipated that they would have a "more brilliant success in the Old World than they have yet met with in the New."

Neither the Alexis play nor the European tour materialized. To replace Buntline, Cody hired Major John ("Arizona John") Burke, who had had many years of experience in the theater. Burke joined Cody originally as manager of Guiseppina Morlacchi. But it was Cody's reference to Hickok that attracted most attention. It had been almost four years since the pair had parted, following the Carr-Penrose expedition of 1868–69. Hickok had furthered his reputation and

BUFFALO Bill and friends in hunting garb. Armed with Remington rolling-block rifles, they are from left to right standing: Elisha Green; "Scott," a New York hatter; and Eugene Overton. Seated are Texas Jack and Buffalo Bill. Although credited to a Denver photographer, we think the plate was made at Omaha ca. July 1873. The Omaha Daily Republican of July 31, 1873, noted that Currier (a local photographer) "photographed Buffalo Bill and party when they were in the city on their way." There is a plate of this group in civilian dress, too. According to a New York periodical, which published a woodcut of Cody based on this photograph in 1876, the original was made by another Omaha photographer, G. C. Eaton. (Courtesy Buffalo Bill Historical Center)

BUFFALO BILL STILL LIVES!
THE ORIGINAL HERO.
NOTE.—The account in the N. Y. Herald of date Aug.
4, concerning the death of "BUFFALO BILL," has no
reference to W. F. CODY, THE VERITABLE HERO.
HE STILL LIVES!
MR. FRED. G. MAEDER respectfully announces TIME
NEARLY FILLED TILL SPRING for the great Combi-
nation of THE SCOUTS OF THE PLAINS,

HON. WM. F. CODY,

THE ORIGINAL

BUFFALO BILL,

J. B. OMOHUNDRO,

TEXAS JACK,

With the renowned Western Hero,

WILD BILL,

MR. J. B. HICKOK,

• Unparalleled desire of managers to secure the original
exponents of the new era in dramatic performances, Border Life versus Mimic Life! Special contract with the
young American author, Mr. Fred. G. Maeder, for his play
of "BUFFALO BILL," altered and adapted expressly.
New situations, fresh incidents.

FULL CORPS OF INDIANS,

With most elaborate and expensive dresses, just brought
from the Prairies by MR. CODY.
COMPLETE DRAMATIC ORGANIZATION,
And every requirement to make this superior to any ever
offered.
Especial attention is called to the fact that the celebra-
ted WILD BILL has pleased to avail himself of the oppor-
tunity to accompany his old comrade. His duties on the
plains will only permit him to
TRAVEL DURING ONE SEASON.
The undersigned invites proposals from all.
FRED G. MAEDER,
Care of W. F. CODY, Brevoort-place Hotel.
20-11°   Tenth street, near Broadway, New York.

THE New York Clipper *of August 16,*
1873, carried this advertisement advising
music hall managers and others that the pro-
duction Scouts of the Plains *was available*
for booking. Of particular interest is the
claim that Hickok's "duties on the plains"
would permit him to spend only one season
with the troupe. We suspect that the prom-
ised remuneration was far more important to
Wild Bill than was the adulation he would
receive. (Courtesy Melvin A. Schulte)

was already a burgeoning legend with exploits as a deputy U.S. marshal in Kansas
and as a lawman in Hays City and Abilene. When it was widely reported in
March 1873 that he had been killed by
Texans at Fort Dodge, he advised the
press that such reports were premature.
He also accused Ned Buntline of using
most of his adventures for the plot of *Buf-*
falo Bill, King of the Border Men. And to
add insult to injury, Buntline had killed
him off in the story. "Ned Buntline has
been trying to murder me with his pen for
years; having failed is now, so I am told,
trying to have it done by some Texans,
but he has signally failed so far."[43]

Hickok joined the Combination for
Scouts of the Plains in September 1873.
Cody believed he would be a great attraction. But he was no actor and grew to
hate the sham heroics. He delighted in
shooting blanks close to the legs of the
extras so that, instead of dying like "good
Injuns," they leaped about, howling with
pain. Cody warned him to stop or he
would have to leave. In March 1874 in
Rochester, New York, Hickok decided
that he had had enough. Cody and
Omohundro were sorry to see him go, but
they admitted that he was a difficult man
to deal with. As a parting gift they each
gave him $500 and a pair of brand-new
.44 caliber Smith & Wesson revolvers to
use out West.

Cody and Omohundro continued with
the Combination. By 1876 it was much
improved and Cody himself was gaining a
reputation as a character actor. Then

NED BUNTLINE

TRIUMPHANT.

HAVING SECURED, IN ADDITION TO MY

STAR DRAMATIC COMPANY,

TWO OF THE MOST FAMOUS, DARING AND
CELEBRATED

SCOUTS OF THE WEST

THE HEROIC GUIDE
AND THE GREAT HUNTER,

"DASHING CHARLIE,"

LATELY IN THE U. S. ARMY AS SCOUT,
AND THE INTREPID HUNTER,
EXPLORER AND INDIAN FIGHTER,

ARIZONA FRANK,

Fresh from the Apache Warpath, I have also at an immense expense succeeded in engaging

P. T. BARNUM'S

Troupe of Wild Comanche and Kiowa Indians,

FOR MY FULL

FALL, WINTER AND SPRING SEASON,

AS WELL AS MY EUROPEAN TOUR, WHICH LAST
WILL COMMENCE IN

JUNE, 1874.

This unequaled combination of talent, grace, rare
originality, and the wild

HEROES AND BEAUTIES

OF THE FOREST, MOUNTAIN AND BORDER,
Will go before the American people in all the leading
theatres West, South, East and North, at

POPULAR PRICES ONLY.

It is an exhibition of dramatic strength, moral, refined,
yet strange and wonderful, unequaled in the

WIDE WORLD.

ROUTES CONTINUALLY ANNOUNCED IN THE COL-
UMNS OF THIS PAPER.
Every person in this organization is free from intem-
perate habits, which so often mar entertainments and
shock sensibilities.

COL. E. Z. C. JUDSON,

MANAGER AND PROPRIETOR.

CHARLES MELVILLE.

A RARE *copy of the Programme for a per-*
formance of The Scouts of the Plains *in*
which Hickok replaced Buntline. Printed on
light green paper in black type, the reverse
side describes various incidents in the lives of
the three scouts. (Courtesy the late Ethel A.
Hickok)

NED *Buntline ran this advertisement in the*
New York Clipper *on August 16, 1873, in*
the same issue that featured one for Cody's
forthcoming Scouts of the Plains*. Bunt-*
line's rival show offered no real competition.
(Courtesy Melvin A. Schulte) LEFT

DURING *the period that he was with the troupe, Wild Bill Hickok was a great attraction. This rare photograph of him and Eugene Overton was made by Gurney & Son, New York, ca. late 1873 or early 1874. The photograph came to light when a number of old cases in the museum exhibit at Cody were overhauled. It had fallen behind another photograph, probably many years ago. Hickok's jacket is not the "Prince Albert" frockcoat that many have called it but is identical in style to the cutaway version Overton is wearing. Overton later joined Cody's Wild West. (Courtesy Buffalo Bill Historical Center)*

MUSIC HALL!

·ONE NIGHT ONLY!

Friday, Nov. 28th.

The most wonderful combination on Earth ! !

' THE REAL LIVING HEROES

BUFFALO BILL!
(Hon. W. F. CODY.)

TEXAS JACK!
(J. B. Omohundro.)

WILD BILL ! !
(J. B. Hickok.).

A TRIBE OF WILD COMANCHE INDIANS !

THE "PEERLESS" DANSEUSE, VOCALISTE AND COMEDIENNE,

M'lle Marlacchi,

and a powerful company in Robbins' thrilling picture of Western border life, entitled

THE SCOUTS OF THE PLAINS.

POPULAR PRICES............50 & 75 CENTS.

Reserved seats without extra charge at J. H. Peacock's Drug Store.
25-3t   JOHN RICKABY, Agent.

THE *Daily Record of the Times (Wilkes-Barre, Pa.) published this advertisement on November 27, 1873, and an accompanying paragraph announced that the Comanches were in the charge of Buffalo Bill and the rest of "them air fellows as belongs" to the Scouts of the Plains troupe. With a warning to "look out for your scalp" and not offend them, everyone was urged to visit the theater. (Courtesy Melvin A. Schulte)*

THE *Scouts of the Plains and friends. From left to right: Elisha Green, Wild Bill Hickok, Buffalo Bill Cody, Texas Jack Omohundro, and Eugene Overton. It is thought that the original plate was a tintype rather than a wetplate, but the original photographer has not been identified. This print is credited to Robert H. Furman of Rochester, New York, who first appeared in the city directories of 1877. Evidently he copied an existing print. It was learned that Furman later "removed to San Diego, Cal." ca. 1887 (Karl Kabelac to Joseph G. Rosa, February 5, 1986). (Courtesy Buffalo Bill Historical Center)*

ABOVE

WIETING OPERA HOUSE.

Friday & Saturday, March 6th & 7th.
The Original Living Heroes,

BUFFALO BILL,
(Hon. W. F. Cody,)

TEXAS JACK,
(J. B. Omohundro,)

WILD BILL,
(J. B. Hickock,)

And the PEERLESS

MORLACCHI,

In the New Sensational Play entitled

Scouts of the Plains!

The performance will commence with the Peerless Dansuese and Pantomime Actress, Mlle MORLACCHI, in a Comedietta of three beautiful dances and will sing Cavatina from the opera of Ernani.

Reserved seats for sale at Leiter Bros.' music store, commencing on Monday, March 2d. Prices as usual.

mar4d4t6

HARRY MINER, Business Manager.

tragedy struck; in April his son, Kit Carson Cody, was taken ill with scarlet fever. Following Cody's overnight dash to be at his side, the boy died in Cody's arms on the twenty-first. To his sister Julia, Cody poured out his heart, telling her that the boy was "too good for this world. We loved him to[o] dearly he could not stay."[44]

Following Kit's death Cody returned to the Combination, but his heart was no longer in it. He began receiving requests from Colonel Anson Mills to join General Crook's command as a scout in the coming Indian campaign. At first he resisted, but six weeks after Kit's death he closed the season early, telling his audience that he was off to fight real Indians.

In 1868 the U.S. government and the Sioux signed a treaty setting aside nearly forty-three thousand square miles of land as a reservation. The land included the Black Hills (which later formed a part of Dakota Territory and are today a part of South Dakota). The Sioux regarded the place as sacred. When General Custer led a military survey expedition through the region in 1874 and reported the discovery of gold, the country was soon overrun with would-be gold seekers. By early 1876

THE *Syracuse, New York,* Journal *carried several advertisements for Cody's Combination. March 3, 1874, marked one of Hickok's last appearances before he quit the troupe in Rochester. (From the collection of Joseph G. Rosa)* LEFT

a number of illegal townships had sprung up, among them Deadwood.

The tribes further complicated things by wandering from their reservations. The government ordered them to return to their reservations before January 31, 1876, or face the consequences. The Indians, spread all over the region, had no intention of obeying such an order. Troops were then ordered, and by May a full-scale expedition was in preparation. On June 9 Cody rejoined the Fifth Cavalry where he found General Carr eagerly awaiting his arrival. The Fifth Cavalry was not a part of the expedition under General Terry. Terry's command included General Custer and the Seventh Cavalry. It was July 7 before Carr's command learned of Custer's "Last Stand" at Little Big Horn on June 25.

The Fifth Cavalry, meanwhile, was ordered to join Crook's command and march to Fort Laramie. On July 17 at Hat Creek (near present-day Montrose, Nebraska, sometimes called War Bonnet Creek), Cody fought his celebrated duel with the Cheyenne subchief Hay-o-Wei, "Yellow Hand" or "Yellow Hair." During a skirmish with the Cheyenne, Cody and Yellow Hand opened fire on each other. Cody shot the Indian through the leg. The shot also killed Yellow Hand's horse. Cody's own mount stumbled, pitching him from the saddle. Cody then shot the Indian through the head and scalped him. Cody later recalled bounding to his feet, brandishing the topknot, and shouting: "The first scalp for Custer!"[45]

COLONEL *Prentiss Ingraham's* Knight of the Plains *was a major success during the 1878–79 season, and this broadside indicates that in looks at least, Cody fitted the role admirably. (From the collection of Joseph G. Rosa)* ABOVE

THE *only known photograph of Kit Carson Cody, ca. 1876, the year that he died. Although in later years Johnny Baker became almost a son to Buffalo Bill, Kit was never far from his thoughts. (Courtesy Buffalo Bill Historical Center)* LEFT

JOHN *Wallace ("Captain Jack") Crawford in costume. The self-styled "Poet Scout of the Black Hills" was probably a better scout than he was an actor or a poet. He distinguished himself on several occasions during the 1876 Indian war by making some hazardous rides. When Cody returned east in August, Jack replaced him as chief of scouts for the Fifth Cavalry. It was he who brought the news of the Battle of Slim Buttes to Fort Laramie, a distance of three hundred fifty miles that he rode in less than four days. (Courtesy Herb Peck, Jr.)* ABOVE

THIS copy of the Buffalo Bill Combination contract is for one of the company's last seasons (by this time, of course, Cody was involved in his Wild West). It provides us with a graphic description of how the company organized its theaters and local publicity. (Courtesy Mahoning Valley Historical Society)

AN *affluent and fashionable Mr. Cody, ca. 1876–78. The crucifix is unusual, but the long chain looped around his neck to form a watch fob is an affectation that was common at the time. These chains occasionally took the form of strings of beads. (Courtesy Buffalo Bill Memorial Museum)*

For Cody, the remainder of the campaign was an anticlimax. Late in August he was saddened by the news of Hickok's murder at Deadwood on the second at the hands of John ("Jack") McCall, who shot him through the back of the head as he played cards in Saloon no. 10. Convinced that there "was little prospect of any more fighting," he determined to "go East so as soon as possible to organize a new 'Dramatic Combination,' and have a new drama written for me, based upon the Sioux War." Captain Jack Crawford, who had replaced Cody as chief of scouts of the Fifth Cavalry, later joined his new Combination. At Virginia City, Montana, in July 1877, Crawford "shot himself in the groin, inflicting a serious wound." One unsympathetic editor remarked that the event was not without its "counterbalancing advantages, for they had to ring down the curtain."[46]

The Cody-Crawford partnership did not last, and Cody was soon back on his own. Cody and Texas Jack Omohundro had ended their partnership when Cody joined General Carr. In the fall of 1876, Jack and his wife organized their own Combination, in which they were joined by Major John M. Burke. When Jack died in 1880, Burke rejoined Cody.[47]

By 1880 Cody and J. V. Arlington (a former character actor in the Combination) and Colonel Prentiss Ingraham joined forces to produce plays and skits. Cody also contemplated taking his Combination to England but later abandoned the idea. Then, in the summer of 1882,

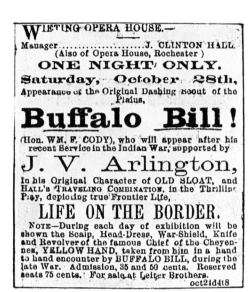

THE *Syracuse, New York, Journal carried this advertisement on October 24, 1876, for Cody's revised Combination. Yellow Hand's scalp was a prominent feature, but it soon disappeared. (From the collection of Joseph G. Rosa)*

at North Platte, he became involved in a local Fourth-of-July celebration described as the "Old Glory Blow-Out," which had cowboys, Indians, and all the spectacle that would soon become an essential part of the "Wild West." It attracted a large audience.

Some months before, Cody had met the actor-manager Nate Salsbury, who had suggested that he expand his stage production to include live animals. Cody was impressed both by Salsbury and by his ideas. Although he did not realize it, he was now on the threshold of his greatest fame.

Notes

1 Don Russell, *The Lives and Legends of Buffalo Bill* (Norman, Okla., 1960; hereafter cited as Russell, *Lives*), 3–5.

2 Ibid., 3.

3 Don Russell, ed., "Julia Goodman's Memoirs of Buffalo Bill" (hereafter cited as Russell, "Julia Memoirs"), *The Kansas Historical Quarterly* 28, no. 4 (Winter 1962): 476–477.

4 Ibid., 484; Joseph G. Rosa, *They Called Him Wild Bill: The Life and Adventures of James Butler Hickok* (Norman, Okla., 1974; hereafter cited as Rosa, *Wild Bill*), 22–27.

5 William F. Cody, *The Life of the Hon. William F. Cody, Known as Buffalo Bill* (Hartford, Conn., 1879; hereafter cited as Cody, *Life*), 135; Records of the Seventh Kansas Volunteer Cavalry Regiment, Archives Division, Kansas State Historical Society (KSHS).

6 Records of the Seventh Kansas Volunteer Cavalry, KSHS.

7 Russell, *Lives*, 78.

8 Cody, *Life*, 152.

9 Records of Fort Hays, Letters Dispatched (1867), microfilm copy, Manuscripts Department, KSHS.

10 Cody, *Life*, 151–152; Russell, *Lives*, 85.

11 Had Cody really killed twelve buffalo a day (every day, that is) for eighteen months, the total would have been about 6,500 buffalo. We suspect that he included some of his freelance kills for sale in and around Hays City in his published total.

12 Joseph G. Rosa, "J. B. Hickok, Deputy U.S. Marshal," *Kansas History: A Journal of the Central Plains* 2, no. 4 (Winter 1979): 239–240.

13 Cody, *Life*, 175–177.

14 Col. George A. Armes, *Ups and Downs of an Army Officer* (Washington, D.C., 1900), 271–272, 292–294.

15 Gen. Philip H. Sheridan, *Personal Memoirs*, 2 vols. (New York, 1888), 2: 300–301.

16 Mrs. Frank C. Montgomery, "Fort Wallace and Its Relation to the Frontier," *Kansas State Historical Society Collections* 17 (1926–28): 230–232; Paul Andrew Hutton, *Phil Sheridan and His Army* (Lincoln, Nebr., and London, 1985), 45–48.

17 Records of Fort Hays, *Leavenworth Times and Conservative*, October 8, 1868.

18 Gen. E. A. Carr, "Carr's Campaign of 1868–69," ms. supplied by Prof. James T. King, 2.

19 Ibid., 31.

20 Report of Bvt. Maj. Gen. E. A. Carr, Commanding Expedition from Fort Lyon, of the Operations of his Command during the Late Campaign against Hostile Indians, Fort Lyon, April 7, 1869, Record Group No. 393 (Department of the Missouri, Letters Received), National Archives, Washington, D.C.

21 Cody, *Life*, 229–233.

22 Ibid., 233–242.

23 Russell, *Lives*, 123.

24 Carr, "Carr's Campaign," 89.

25 Cody, *Life*, 260–261.

26 Henry E. Davies, *Ten Days on the Plains* (New York, 1871), 26.

27 Ibid., 25–26, 66.

28 Cody, *Life*, 171–174.

29 Mrs. Frank C. Montgomery, "Fort Wallace," 226; Kenneth J. Almy, ed., "Thof's Dragon and the Letters of Capt. Theophilus H. Turner, M.D., U.S. Army," *Kansas History: A Journal of the Central Plains* 10, no. 3 (Autumn 1987): 185–186.

30 The Kansas State Historical Society conducted an intensive search into the Cody-Comstock contest some years ago but was unable to find any contemporary references apart from Cody's 1879 autobiography.

31 Whistler, Handsmeller, and Badger, three leaders of the cut-off band of Oglala Sioux, were murdered in the fall of 1872 somewhere on the Republican River. Investigations by the army early in 1873 revealed that those responsible were whites who formed part of what was called "Wild Bill's outfit." Some thought that this was Hickok, but official and public records laid the blame on Mortimer N. Kress, known locally as "Wild Bill of the Blue River" to distinguish him from his famous namesake. (Rosa, *Wild Bill*, 207–221.)

32 Russell, *Lives*, 176.

33 Cody, *Life*, 301.

34 Ibid., 310–311.

35 Russell, *Lives,* 186–187.

36 Cody, *Life,* 277–278.

37 Russell, *Lives,* 192; Louisa Frederici Cody (in collaboration with Courtney Ryley Cooper), *Memories of Buffalo Bill* (New York and London, 1920), 232.

38 *Cleveland Herald* (1879?), undated clipping in the Cody Scrapbooks, Buffalo Bill Museum, Cody, Wyoming.

39 *Chicago Times,* December 15, 1872; *Chicago Daily Tribune,* December 18, 1872.

40 This fact was not lost on the press, which repeatedly emphasized that Cody and Omohundro were genuine.

41 Herschel C. Logan, *Buckskin and Satin* (Harrisburg, Pa., 1954), 83.

42 Undated clipping from the *Missouri Democrat,* Cody Scrapbooks.

43 Mendota, Illinois *Bulletin,* April 11, 1873.

44 Stella Adelyne Foote, *Letters from "Buffalo Bill"* (Billings, Mont., 1954), 13.

45 Cody, *Life,* 343–344.

46 *Leavenworth Daily Times,* July 15, 1877.

47 Russell, *Lives,* 233, 247, 296.

2

THE WILD WEST

The origin of the Wild West Show or Exhibition in America is disputed. Doc Carver claimed that he "invented" it, while others believe that Wild Bill Hickok's Grand Buffalo Hunt at Niagara Falls was the first such venture. Carver's claim was utterly without foundation, and Hickok's contribution to the Niagara Falls event was not as its organizer but as master of ceremonies. So we must look elsewhere to gain some insight into the origins of what would eventually become a household word on two continents.

A number of people contributed to the Wild West Show. In 1843 the Great Barnum purchased fifteen starved and weary buffalo calves, all about one year old, from C. D. French, an expert rider and lasso artist. Barnum's $700 purchase price also included French's services to look after and help exhibit the animals. Barnum's "Grand Buffalo Hunt" at Hoboken, New Jersey, that same year included Indian dancers and attracted twenty-four thousand people. It was reported that the buffalo escaped and the crowd panicked, and at least one man was killed and others injured. Undeterred, in 1860 Barnum became a partner in James Capen ("Grizzly") Adams's California Menagerie, and in various parts of the East and West, exhibitions featuring cowboys and Indians were welcome.

In 1868 Joseph G. McCoy, in an effort to attract Texas cattlemen and to promote the newly established rail link between Chicago and Abilene, Kansas, loaded wild horses, three buffalo, and two elk onto a railroad car. Accompanied by two Mexicans from California, a Kansan named Thompson, and several assistants, he visited several cities en route to Chicago. This Wild West type of exhibit proved very successful, and McCoy followed it up by organizing a "Grand Excursion to the Far West! A Wild and Exciting Chase after the Buffalo, on his Native Plain." Aimed primarily at those engaged in the cattle business, it attracted a large number of sportsmen. McCoy supplied horses and camp equipment. People were advised to "bring their own firearms."[1]

Spectacular though such events were, they were never intended to be long-term. Indeed it might be said that Cody's "Old Glory Blow-Out" in 1882 would have shared a similar fate but for the man himself and his fortuitous meeting with Nate Salsbury that same year. Salsbury, an experienced and popular actor-manager, had toyed with such a venture as early as 1876. Having visited Australia, he seriously considered using Australian

WILD *Bill Hickok's appearance at Niagara Falls in Sidney Barnett's Grand Buffalo Hunt proved to be a financial flop for Barnett, but he and others appreciated the lure of such a personality. This reproduction was made from a copy of an original broadside found hanging on a barn wall some years ago in Ontario. (Courtesy Archives of Ontario, Canada)*

GRAND
BUFFALO HUNT!
AT
NIAGARA FALLS,
ON THE
28th and 30th August, 1872.

THE BUFFALOES CAPTURED FOR THIS PURPOSE NEAR THE FOOT OF THE

ROCKY MOUNTAINS,

After one of the most exciting chases ever witnessed on the plains, will be liberated in a

LARGE AND BEAUTIFUL PARK AT NIAGARA FALLS,
CANADA SIDE.

This Park has been specially made for the purpose, the portion set apart for spectators is secured from the slightest danger by fences strong enough to resist an elephant.

This Novel and most exciting affair will be under the direction and management of the most celebrated Scout and Hunter of the great plains

Mr. Wm. HICKOK

better known as **WILD BILL**, of whom General Custar says "whether on foot or on horse back, he is one of the most perfect types of physical manhood I ever saw and then, as now, the most famous scout on the plains.

Notwithstanding the refusal of the Commissioner of Indian Affairs at Washington to allow the Pawnee Indians engaged by me to leave their reservation, and which caused the postponement of the Hunt on a former occasion, though the expenditure of a large amount of money I have secured the services of some of the

INDIANS OF THE BEST HUNTING BAND
Of the Sacs and Fox Tribes;

And they will appear in full War Costume, mounted on fleet ponies brought from the plains.

Over fifty Indians of different tribes will appear on the field in full War Dress, and take part in the Hunt, presenting a most unique and beautiful spectacle.

The Sac and Fox and other Indians mounted will display their splendid Horsemanship, pursuing the Buffaloes as they dash headlong over the grassy plain, and with prodigious strength and unerring aim will send their feathery arrows at the flying animals, pursuing them a great distance and exhibiting all the singular and daring feats peculiar to Buffalo Hunting in the Great West, where this wild and ferocious monarch of the plains roams in millions.

The Mexican Vaquero Troupe,

Comprising the band of Lasso Men mounted on their Mustang ponies will attack the buffaloes, and with dexterous throws of the Lariat capture them, they will also exhibit

THEIR WONDERFUL FEATS
WITH THE LARIAT IN CAPTURING AND THROWING

WILD TEXAS CATTLE.

AMPLE ROOM HAS BEEN PROVIDED FOR

FIFTY THOUSAND SPECTATORS.

Arrangements have been made with the different Railroads to run

EXCURSION TRAINS AT GREATLY REDUCED RATES OF FARE,
Allowing ample time to see the hunt and the Falls.

This colossal undertaking in which neither trouble nor expense have been spared. The public may rely upon being a perfect success and a genuine affair.

Thousands and thousands of Dollars have been expended in transporting the outfit from the Great Plains, a distance of near two thousand miles.

The opportunity for seeing such a magnificent affair may never occur again and no person should miss the opportunity now first offered of witnessing the most interesting, the most exciting, and the most thrilling spectacle ever beheld East of the Missouri River, as well as the boldest undertaking of the kind ever attempted, requiring energy, skill, courage and capital.

The price of Admission will be only 50 Cents.

Hunt to commence at 3 o'clock, p.m.

The 44th Regimental Band will be present.
SIDNEY BARNETT.

"jockeys" in place of American cowboys and Mexican vaqueros. But he changed his mind when he realized that the more colorful cowboys and vaqueros would have a greater appeal to Americans. When he mentioned his idea to Cody, he had already made up his mind that "Buffalo Bill" was a big drawing card, that Cody had the experience, skill, and fame to attract audiences. His belief was strengthened when he visited England and learned that dime novels featuring "Buffalo Bill" were for sale and that the scout was already a hero. Cody was enthusiastic, but at that time neither individual had the finances to promote the scheme, so it was temporarily abandoned. Therefore, it came as a great shock to Salsbury when, in the spring of 1883, Cody telegraphed him to offer him a share in his Wild West, which Cody had organized in association with Doc Carver—provided, of course, Carver did not object. Salsbury, who regarded Carver as a "fakir," was both angry and saddened by Cody's rashness in going ahead without him, so he declined Cody's offer. Later he commented that Cody and Carver "went on the road and made a ghastly failure."[2]

Cody had met Carver in New York during his 1882–83 season, and they reminisced over their experiences in North Platte, Fort McPherson, and the surrounding country. Carver was by this time an internationally known marksman. In later years he invented an early life for himself that was not only remarkable, but so falsified as to cast doubt upon his known abilities. Born to William and Deborah Carver in Winslow, Illinois, on May 7, 1840, he later claimed that his father so abused him that he ran away when a child and headed West, where he lived for some time with the Santee Sioux. His extraordinary marksmanship, credited by the Indians to his Spirit Gun, was further enhanced when he shot a white buffalo and an elusive old gray or "silver" elk. The Indians concluded that only an Evil Spirit could have accomplished such a feat. Carver then proclaimed himself the "Evil Spirit of the Plains."[3]

The truth, of course, is less dramatic. William Frank Carver was educated in Winslow, Illinois, and later trained by his father as a dentist. By the time he headed West, however, he was already a marksman. In July or August 1872 he reached Fort McPherson, where he practiced dentistry for a while before moving to a claim on the Medicine Creek. Here he became acquainted with a number of well-known frontier personalities, including Cody and Texas Jack. He also shot against the frontier's foremost woman "shootist," Ena Raymond. She taught him nothing about shooting, but he taught her the rudiments of dentistry, which she apparently practiced upon her friends. On one occasion, she recalled, a tooth that she had "hammered" for Texas Jack gave him some trouble![4]

Early in 1874 Carver brought his

WILLIAM *Frank ("Doc") Carver, self-styled Champion Rifle Shot of the World. From a photograph made by Negretti & Zambra, London, 1879. (Courtesy William B. Secrest)*

brother (curiously, also christened William) and mother to live with him on his claim on the Medicine. By October, however, Carver was again on the move. He left Nebraska for Cheyenne, Wyoming, where he remained for some months before disappearing. By his own account he moved to California and from there began a remarkable shooting career as the self-styled Champion Rifle Shot of the World. He visited parts of Europe and established a formidable reputation in England as a shot. Although the latter part of his life is well documented, his alleged western adventures are not. Some time before his death he produced a manuscript in which he claimed to have been involved in adventures with Wild Bill Hickok and other frontier personalities. He fooled one well-known writer (Raymond W. Thorp) into believing every word and publishing a fictionalized biography that is still controversial.[5]

When Carver again met up with Cody in 1883, he was already teamed up with Captain Adam Bogardus, an excellent exhibition shot, who readily agreed to appear in the proposed Cody-Carver venture. Later, Carver was to claim that the Wild West was entirely his idea and that he had originally wanted to call it The

THE *cast of the original Wild West ca. 1883, photographed by W. Phillippi & Bro., Philadelphia. Standing to Cody's right is Johnny Baker, and again to his right (next to the man with the straw hat) is Major Frank* *North. Dominating the front row, and surrounded by members of his family, is the ubiquitous figure of John Nelson. (Courtesy Buffalo Bill Memorial Museum)*

Golden West. Cody, however, took it upon himself to change the name to "Cody & Carver's Wild West." Temperamentally, the two were entirely unsuited for such a partnership, but their individual talents overcame personal differences.

Cody, ever anxious for authenticity, telegraphed Luke Voorhees, manager of the Cheyenne and Black Hills Stage Line, and asked him for a Concord stagecoach. Luke duly obliged and sent him the coach in which Cody had originally ridden in 1876. When new, the coach had cost the company $1,800. Having lain abandoned for three months follow-

ing an Indian attack, it was no longer in pristine condition, but it had been rescued, repaired, and placed back in service. It was to remain a star attraction of the Wild West during the exhibition's entire existence.[6]

Cody and Carver decided to stage the first performance of their Wild West at Omaha, Nebraska. Cody's arrival on May 12, 1883, in company with Major Frank North and thirty-six Pawnee Indians—including squaws and children—caused a ripple of excitement in the crowd at the depot. Dan Clother, who had gathered the Indians together, introduced Cody to them. There was a vigorous "How! How!" from the Indians, and they gathered around to shake hands with him. Buffalo Bill then produced a large box of cigars, which were hastily passed around.

Cody informed the press that ten Sioux Indians were also expected to arrive, making the Indian contingent about sixty. The Indians would carry their own tepees and implements, and there would be little change in their normal way of life. There was also "good medicine" in the form of a buffalo calf, "Western Lilly," that had been born in the encampment.

Buffalo Bill also noted that "forty odd thousand dollars" had already been spent getting the entertainment together and the figure would soon reach fifty thousand, not including transportation, printing costs, salaries, or daily provisions. Nevertheless, he and his partner had high hopes of success.

The Wild West opened on May 17 to an estimated audience of eight thousand people. It was an immediate success. "Cody's Cyclone, the 'Wild West,'" remarked the press, "sweeps all victoriously before it," and the crowd determined that it was indeed a "go." A twenty-piece band led the opening parade and was followed by "Little Standing Bull" replete with headdress and warpaint and riding a pony. Behind him rode three Pawnees; then came three grown buffalo and a newborn calf, "a frisky young thing." More mounted Indians followed, and then came Buffalo Bill and Carver ac-

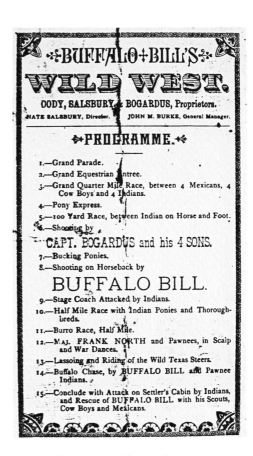

AN *early version of the Wild West program. (Courtesy Mahoning Valley Historical Society)*

companied by cowboys, some other animals, and the Deadwood Stage drawn by six fine mules, and last, another band.

"Pop" Whitaker, a noted caller at athletic games as far away as New York, announced and described all the acts. It is most unlikely that the audience realized that it was witnessing a preview of what would become standard fare in the Wild

West—the Pony Express; the attack on the Deadwood stagecoach (saved in the nick of time by Cody and Carver and a party of scouts); an exhibition shooting by Carver, Bogardus, and Cody, "the three best shots in the United States and the champion shot of the world." The final act was a "buffalo chase." At the end Cody made a speech, which was greeted with tremendous applause, especially when he announced that the enterprise was a "thoroughbred Nebraska show," in which they should "hold the mirror up to nature." If there had been any doubts before, there were certainly none now. The Wild West was a success.[7]

Nate Salsbury kept a watchful eye on the progress of "Cody & Carver's Wild West" (or "The Wild West, Hon. W. F. Cody and Dr. W. F. Carver's Rocky Mountain and Prairie Exhibition" as it

was sometimes called), for he realized that it could not last. Both men had reputations as drinkers, but it was Carver who suffered the ill temper so often associated with excessive consumption. At Coney Island on one occasion he missed his shots, and, enraged, he smashed his rifle over his horse's ears and then struck his assistant. It did not help when the press began singling out Cody for praise, for it was quickly appreciated that Cody was the real westerner and Carver the poseur.

There were other problems, too. The buffalo-roping competition, when a number of half-wild buffalo were turned loose in the arena and roped and ridden by cowboys, was hazardous. One bull, Monarch, was always ignored until finally Buffalo Bill ordered him roped and ridden, and a reluctant pair, Buck Taylor and Jim Lawson, roped and threw him. However, when both men refused to climb aboard, Cody himself did the honors. He stayed on for a few minutes but was finally thrown so heavily that he ended up in the hospital for a couple of weeks. When he rejoined the show in Chicago, Gordon Lillie, alias "Pawnee Bill," who was a member of the troupe during its early period recalled that Cody, a wiser man now, substituted a simulated "Buffalo Chase, by Buffalo Bill and the Pawnee Indians" in place of what could easily have been his last ride.[8]

In Chicago Cody learned that Nate Salsbury was appearing in the city in a play, so he hastened to see him. Cody begged Salsbury to take over the exhibition, for he was through with Carver and could not face "another summer for a hundred thousand dollars." The pair just could not get along. Before any decision could be made, Cody was called home because of the illness of his eleven-year-old daughter Orra Maude. Her death and yet another falling out with his wife, who threatened divorce, left him in low spirits. The final confrontation with Carver came when Doc proposed a winter tour. Cody flatly refused. At Omaha, ironically the place where the partnership had begun, the partners closed their season and divided their physical assets by the flip of a coin. Fortunately Buffalo Bill kept the Deadwood coach.[9]

Replacing Cody with Jack Crawford, Doc Carver carried on with his part of the Wild West. He visited Canada in 1884, and in New England in 1885 he and Cody clashed. This confrontation led to a court action. Carver claimed that he won his case, but he lost his show. In 1886 he joined forces with W. W. Cole's New Colossal Show and for a brief period the circus of Adam Forepaugh, Jr., as well. A revived Carver's Wild West visited Europe in 1889 and Australia in 1890 and 1891. In 1892 Carver introduced a program in which he gave the Wild West outdoors in the afternoon and a melodrama called *The Scout* in the evening. The same company appeared in both performances.

Long after his show business appearances, Carver displayed a bitter hatred toward Cody, for despite his acknowledged ability with a rifle, he lacked Cody's presence and true-life exploits. Perhaps this inferiority explains his reliance on fiction in an effort to present himself in a better light. He died on August 31, 1927, in Sacramento, California, and his body was returned to Winslow, Illinois, where he was buried beside his mother on September 5.[10]

Now at last in 1883 Cody and Salsbury joined forces, with Bogardus as their partner. The contract was drawn up by John Peter Algeld, governor of Illinois when the Wild West made its celebrated appearance on the outskirts of the Chicago Exposition in 1893 as "Buffalo Bill's Wild West—America's National Entertain-

THE *indefatigable Major John ("Arizona John") Burke, Cody's erstwhile theatrical manager-cum-actor turned press agent. Tentatively dated ca. 1880, this Anderson portrait was probably made at Staten Island in 1886. (Courtesy Buffalo Bill Historical Center)*

ment." Both Cody and Salsbury would later claim to have thought of the show, but it is hard not to believe Salsbury's long account of its beginnings. There seems to have been an inevitability about its birth, a show business marriage of two men who complemented each other, and who in their different ways were at home in surroundings as different as Windsor Castle and small towns in Wisconsin and Florida. The fourth member of the team was John Burke, business manager and, according to Russell, the "greatest of press agents."[11]

Salsbury's comments, published long after his death, attest to a relationship that was less brotherly than it had appeared to be. Salsbury was born in Illinois in 1846. He was discharged from the Union army—he was a drummer boy— because of his age. He later re-enlisted. Wounded and taken prisoner, he is said to have ended the war rich because of his prowess at poker in Andersonville. He became an actor, ran the Salsbury Troubadors, wrote plays for the company, and toured widely in English-speaking countries. He married a beautiful English soprano, Rachel Samuels. In Australia, inspired by the local races, he conceived

of an outdoor show. Discussions with an Australian gave him the idea of a Wild West show. In 1884 he became vice president and general manager of the Wild West, though he continued to run his Troubadors for a time. By the 1890s he was living in great style on Ninety-third Street near Central Park.[12]

When Cody and Salsbury first met in New York in 1882, both were acting there. Clearly, Salsbury saw Cody as a figurehead rather than as comanager. The partners agreed that Salsbury should return to Europe the following summer and cash in on Cody's fame in Britain and Europe. Burke, whose job was to promote Cody and the Wild West, found little favor in Salsbury's eyes. Salsbury's attitude derived partly from his belief that it suited Burke and other Cody "hero-worshipers" who depended on the great man's goodwill, to make Cody, not Salsbury, the originator of the show, so that they could "edge their feeble claims to being an integral part" of its success. Salsbury also believed that Burke and company had not forgiven him for taking over the reins of the show. Whether this was a constant belief or an occasional perception is impossible to say, but it must be noted as a background to what happened. Like all partnerships, this hugely successful one had its strains.[13] Nate Salsbury went to St. Louis early in 1884 to see what he had become involved with. He was not happy with what he found—"a lot of harpies [including Cody] called old-timers" getting drunk at Cody's expense.

Salsbury's letter had a great effect on Cody, who wrote back a repentant apology:

> Your very sensible and truly rightful letter has just been read and it has been the means of showing me just where I stand. And I solemnly promise you that after this you will never see me under the influence of liquor. I may have to take two or three drinks today to brace up on; that will be all as long as we are partners. I appreciate all you have done. Your judgement and business is good and from this on I will do my work to the letter. This drinking surely ends today and your pard will be himself, and on deck all the time.[14]

Cody kept his promise reasonably well, it seems, but it made poor copy. A series of tall-story tellers assigned Nate Salsbury to limit Cody to one drink a day, for which Cody allegedly used a schooner. Gene Fowler expanded the lie to the extent of a dozen drinks a day in twelve mighty tumblers. The stories multiplied. They were harmless perhaps, but they were basically unfair to a showman who became truly professional. How much drink Cody put away after a season was over is another matter, but the authors are unaware of any performance's being affected by Cody's drinking from the start of the Wild West proper to his final retirement.[15]

The 1884 company was a strong one. Buck Taylor, King of the Cowboys, was destined to become the star cowboy; indeed, the word "cowboy" was rehabilitated by Cody. Since the mid-eighteenth century, when New York Colony's landowners so described their rebellious tenantry, the word had suffered from negative connotations. In the American Revolution, cowboys were Loyalist guerrillas who stole Patriot cows, and as the word headed west it remained uncomplimentary. "A band of armed desperadoes known as 'Cowboys'" were, President Arthur claimed in his annual message to Congress in 1881, "menaces to the peace of Arizona Territory." It was Cody who reclaimed the breed in the ears and eyes of Americans, and Taylor was Cody's instrument. In case patrons were nervous about the six-foot five-inch, wild, albeit handsome, lasso-throwing "critter," they were assured that he was as "amiable as a child." Audiences could watch him work without sympathizing with the animals.[16]

Buck Taylor got billing, as did Frank North. Unfortunately North suffered a tragic accident in Hartford, Connecticut, when his saddle cinch broke. He was thrown from his horse and trampled by another one. After a long spell in the hospital he rejoined the Wild West but had to leave again. He died in March 1885. Con Groner, the Cow-Boy Sheriff of the Platte, was another performer with billing. A number of experts rode bucking horses. A new and ever popular act this season was to be "Attack on Settler's Cabin by Indians and Rescue by Buffalo Bill with His Scouts, Cowboys and Mexicans." Indians were signed up for a year.

WILLIAM *Levi ("Buck") Taylor stood six feet five inches tall in his socks, and his great height, combined with his matinee-idol looks, made him a natural for the Wild West. He learned his craft at Cody's Nebraska ranch and later, as King of the Cowboys, he enthralled audiences worldwide. This photograph by Anderson of New York is believed to have been made on Staten Island in 1886. (Courtesy Buffalo Bill Historical Center)*

Johnny Baker.

ANOTHER *Anderson plate made on Staten Island in 1886. Johnny Baker was about seventeen years of age when this photograph was made. Compare the dress of the cowboys with the later styles affected after the turn of the century. (Courtesy Buffalo Bill Memorial Museum)* ABOVE

NAPOLEON *Sarony of New York made a number of plates of Buffalo Bill, but we think this is one of the best and certainly the most dramatic. The photograph was taken on Staten Island in 1886. (Courtesy Buffalo Bill Historical Center)* OPPOSITE

Cody's record with his Indians was excellent throughout his career.[17]

The 1884 season opened in St. Louis in April. It was "vastly enlarged and reorganized" and played to excellent crowds there, as well as in Chicago and New York, but the one-day stands proved uneconomical. The show was taken to the

World's Industrial and Cotton Exposition in New Orleans that winter. Alas, Salsbury was needed, but he was performing with his Troubadors. Back at the Wild West, however, Cody had unwisely given the job of renting show grounds and booking shows to Pony Bob Haslam, a famous Pony Express rider and one of his

WE *suspect that although tentatively dated 1883, this photograph was made ca. 1886* *and is possibly another by Sarony. (Courtesy Buffalo Bill Historical Center)*

friends. Haslam hired a steamboat (of sorts) that collided with another steamboat near Rodney Island, Mississippi. Although the Deadwood Stage was saved, equipment, arms, the bandwagon, and some animals perished. Miraculously, no lives were lost, though it was claimed that the river was eight feet deep at that point.[18]

Salsbury, meanwhile, was playing in Denver, where he received from Cody a telegraph message that ranks high among show business disaster messages: "OUTFIT AT BOTTOM OF THE RIVER, WHAT DO YOU ADVISE?" Nate, the complete professional, told the orchestra leader to re-

peat the overture. He wanted to think. Finally he sent this message: "GO TO NEW ORLEANS, REORGANIZE, AND OPEN ON YOUR DATE." Then he went on stage. The message inspired Cody to become a true theatrical organizer; in just over a week he procured more buffalo and elk, along with transport and other equipment, and he was able to open on time.[19]

This feat deserved a little luck for the company. Instead, it rained for forty-four days. Cody obeyed the show business dictum that the show must go on, however small the audience, though to play, as he did, to just nine ticketholders on one occasion was conduct beyond the call of duty. By the end of the winter the show was in debt to the lamentable tune of $60,000, and it was at this unhappy time that news came of Major North's untimely death. Cody wrote to Salsbury that he would do his best for one more season before going on a "drunk that is a drunk." Until then he would be "staunch and true."

Cody continued to make plans. Young Johnny Baker, virtually an adopted son since he had started trailing after the great man back in North Platte, was now, Cody wrote Salsbury, "shooting fit to beat L." Cody was going to make him a star.

At this time a superstar, Phoebe Anne Moses, better known as Annie Oakley, appeared on the scene.[20] Born in 1860 in an Ohio log cabin, one of a family of eight, by the time she was seven she had lost a father and a stepfather. At eight she started shooting to feed the family. Her fame as a markswoman became so great that at fifteen she was put up to challenge Frank Butler, a notable shot. As the millions who have enjoyed *Annie Get Your Gun* know, Oakley defeated Butler. For dramatic reasons the great Irving Berlin show distorts facts and keeps the pair apart. In fact, a year after they met they embarked on a marriage of legendary happiness. Butler soon gave up his own considerable career to act as his wife's manager.[21]

Cody and Salsbury were not overeager to take on the Butlers at first; they had too many shooting acts already. However, at this point Bogardus left the show, and

Butler suggested that he and Annie be given a three-day trial at Louisville. Annie later said, "I went right in and did my best before 17,000 people and was engaged in fifteen minutes." Cody introduced her to his company: "This little Missie here is Miss Annie Oakley. She's to be the only white woman with our show. And I want you boys to welcome her and protect her," a request that no decent Victorian male could refuse. Cody called her "Little Missie" and Salsbury immediately gave her billing, a very rare honor with the Wild West. She never had or needed a contract. Her frail appearance contrasted strikingly with most of the company. Annie came on like an ingenue, tripping along and blowing kisses. Fellows and Freeman noted the way she set audiences at ease, preparing them for the continual firing that followed. Only they have managed to dent her image a little, criticizing her for being a tightwad who did not join the rest of the gang in town. True or not, it can only have improved her performances.[22]

The Peerless Wing and Rifle Shot, as she was billed, was also said to be a fine rider, "and her success with the public has been greatly enhanced by the fact that in dress, style, and execution she is as original as she is attractive." More important, of course, was her prowess. The 1893 program made that very clear:

The first two years before the public she devoted to Rifle and Pistol Shooting, and there is very little in that line

ANNIE *Oakley photographed by Gilbert &* *Bacon, Philadelphia, ca. 1889. In her right* *hand she is holding a Stevens tip-up single-* *shot rifle (caliber unknown) with walnut* *fore-end and stock. Lying against a rock is a* *Stevens target pistol. To Annie's left are a* *shotgun and a rifle. (Courtesy Buffalo Bill* *Historical Center)*

she has not accomplished. At Tiffin, Ohio, she once shot a ten-cent piece held between the thumb and forefinger of an attendant at a distance of 30 feet. In April, 1884, she attempted to beat the best record made at balls thrown in the air—the best record was 984 by Dr. Ruth. Miss OAKLEY used a Stevens' 22 cal. rifle and broke 943. In February, 1885, she attempted the feat of shooting 5,000 balls in one day, loading the guns herself. In this feat she used three 16-gauge hammer guns; the balls were thrown from three traps 15 yards rise; out of the 5,000 shot at, she broke 4,722; on the second thousand she only missed 16, making *the best* 1,000 ball record, 984. Besides the thousands of exhibitions she has given in Europe and America, she has shot in over 50 matches and tournaments, winning forty-one prizes; her collection of medals and fire-arms, all of which have been won or presented to her, is considered one of the finest in the world.

Long before Annie reemerged in musical form, she had a singular honor paid her by show business; complimentary tickets were called "Annie Oakleys." The tickets were often punched through the middle to help those counting a show's takings. The great Hunkpapa Sioux Sitting Bull bestowed on her the totally accurate nickname Little Sure Shot. Sitting Bull had joined a number of Sioux for a tour arranged by Colonel Alvaren Allen in 1884. The show was to play in fifteen cities and was advertised as "the slayer of General Custer." Sitting Bull had been promised a meeting with the president, which he did not get. When in St. Paul, Minnesota, he saw Annie Oakley performing in a theater and was so excited by her prowess that he called out, "*Watanya cicilia*"—Little Sure Shot. This enthusiasm would later benefit the Wild West.[23]

It was this season that finally established the shape of the Wild West, which, despite later additions, remained virtually the same until the end and influenced all other such shows. After the wretched weather in New Orleans, success was needed, and it came as a week-long triumph in St. Louis. The *Globe-Democrat* made a significant point: "The most remarkable fact is that among so many thousands there were heard no grumbling nor expressions of dissatisfaction, and those who were present will have nothing but agreeable recollections of the Buffalo Bill Wild West."[24]

The next stop was in Chicago's Driving Park, a two-week engagement beginning May 17. The opening performance

ANNIE *Oakley posing with her L. C. Smith shotgun. At her feet are a Stevens-Gould target pistol and a Smith & Wesson New Model no. 3 revolver. (Courtesy Scout's Rest Ranch)*

attracted more than twenty thousand. The *Chicago Tribune* estimated that this was more than a twentieth of the population, a fraction greater than all the local preachers had attracted that Sunday morning. It helped that General Sherman had praised the show as "wonderfully realistic and historically reminiscent." The realism of the Wild West is a constant theme of reviews through the years and of claims by the management. The term is somewhat suspect, but clearly the Wild West was far more realistic, both visually and in spirit, than were any of its rivals. There were four other Wild Wests that year, and Cody criticized their claims and the use of the words "Wild West." A complicated copyright title was used—*The Wild West or Life among the Red Man and the Road Agents of the Plains and Prairies—An Equine Dramatic Exposition on Grass or Under Canvas, of the Adventures of Frontiersmen and Cowboys.* This and the original 1883 copyright are essential in understanding the nature of the Wild West in its spring glory.[25]

Cody copyrighted the Wild West according to an Act of Congress on December 22, 1883, and registered a typescript at the Library of Congress on June 1, 1885. Some features spanned the entire history of what the deposited copy called

BUFFALO BILL'S "WILD WEST"
PRAIRIE EXHIBITION,
AND ROCKY MOUNTAIN SHOW,
A DRAMATIC-EQUESTRIAN
EXPOSITION
OF
LIFE ON THE PLAINS,
WITH ACCOMPANYING MONOLOGUE
AND
INCIDENTAL MUSIC
THE WHOLE INVENTED AND
ARRANGED BY
W. F. CODY
W. F. CODY AND N. SALSBURY,
PROPRIETORS AND MANAGERS
WHO HEREBY CLAIM AS THEIR
SPECIAL
PROPERTY THE VARIOUS EFFECTS INTRODUCED IN
THE PUBLIC PERFORMANCES
OF
BUFFALO BILL'S "WILD WEST"[26]

The cowboy band, suitably attired in western gear with white hats, entertained the gathering crowd. Frank Richmond took his place in a judge's box and, as master of ceremonies, used his magnificent voice to introduce the proceedings. He spurned the idea that the "exhibition" was the result of "what is technically called 'rehearsals.'" Any observer would see that "men and animals alike are the creatures of circumstances, depending for their success upon their own skill, daring and sagacity."[27]

First came the grand processional, with

THE *original of this photograph measures 9½ by 14½ inches and bears the penciled comment on the reverse "Wm. Cody (Buffalo Bill) and Pawnee Indians." It has been established, however, that it was made by Anderson at Staten Island in 1886. To Cody's right are Pawnee scouts and to his left Sioux chiefs. From left to right they are Brave Chief, Eagle Chief, Knife Chief, Young Chief, Cody, American Horse, Rocky Bear, Flies Above, and Long Wolf. Flies Above, Rocky Bear, and Long Wolf traveled to Europe with Cody, and several others in the group came over in 1887. Long Wolf died in London in June 1892 and is buried in West Brompton Cemetery, a stone's throw from Earl's Court (Paul Fees to Joseph G. Rosa, January 15, 1982). (From the collection of Joseph G. Rosa)*

Richmond introducing each act. In 1885 the Pawnee contingent appeared first, followed by their chief, White Eagle. Then came the Mexican vaqueros, followed by the Wichitas, led by "Dave." In came the cowboys followed by Buck Taylor, then

Con Groner, the sheriff who had "tamed" the North Platte area and certainly looked bold enough, covered with pistols, bowie knives, and a rifle. Then it was the turn of the Sioux warriors. After that came the star of stars, who had been chief of scouts of the United States Army under ten generals "and others." After more stirring words, including a mention of the "lamented Custer," Richmond's stentorian tones hailed "the Honorable William F. Cody, 'Buffalo Bill.'" A bugle sounded, and Cody entered on his horse "Charlie" (affectionately known by all as "Old Charlie"). In his fine voice Richmond welcomed the audience to the equestrian part of the exhibition, then turned to the company and called out: "Wild West, are you ready? Go!"[28]

First on the bill was a quarter-mile horse race featuring a cowboy, an Indian, and a Mexican. Then came the Pony Express feature, which would be maintained throughout the Wild West's history. This accurately showed the switch of rider and his "mochilla"—containing the mail pouches—from one horse to another. (Bill Johnson's alleged nonstop ride of 240 miles over the plains and the ride of 310 miles in twenty-six hours and forty-five minutes may be considered show business "hype.") The next act was a 100-yard race between two Indians, one on foot, the other on horseback. Then came the famous recreation of the duel between Cody and Yellow Hand. The arena was full of cowboys and Indians for the scene, and there was a small hill between them. Yellow Hand issued a challenge, Cody took it up, and shots were exchanged as they closed. After fighting mounted, the pair fought on foot, spear versus knife. Moments later, Yellow Hand was well and truly "scalped." The Indians

and cowboys now engaged in a general fight and drove the Indians off.[29]

Now came the moment for marksmanship. Richmond introduced Seth Clover, who would "give an exhibition of his skill, shooting with a Winchester repeating rifle, at composition balls thrown from the hand." Later, he would fire at half dollars, dimes, and nickels, as well as a number of balls. Next on the bill was "Master Johnny Baker," the sixteen-year-old "Cowboy Kid," shooting his rifle from a variety of positions, including leaning backward, over a support, and over his head.[30]

It was Annie Oakley's turn now to shoot at clay pigeons sprung from a trap; to shoot double, from two traps sprung at the same time; to pick up the gun from the ground after the trap was sprung; to shoot double in the same manner; and to shoot three composition balls thrown in the air in rapid succession, the first with the rifle held upside down upon the head, the second and third with the shotgun.[31]

Next came cowboy fun time, or "the riding of bucking ponies and mules by Broncho Bill, Coyote Bill, Bridle Bill," and so on. Tom Clayton's taming of the ferocious mare Dynamite was a high spot, though the story that the beast turned somersaults is somewhat startling. Last came the great Buck Taylor, a high spot among high spots being his picking up both his hat and handkerchief from the ground at full gallop. Then into the arena came Buffalo Bill on horseback.[32]

Hailed as the Champion All-Round

Shot of the World by Richmond, Cody would shoot with shotgun, rifle, and revolver at clay pigeons and composition balls. Cody himself pulled the traps. Next came shooting clay pigeons American style, with the butt of the gun below the elbow; then followed by English style, with the butt below the armpit. Cody then shot clay pigeons in a variety of ways, including holding the weapon with one hand and shooting twenty clay pigeons within one minute and thirty seconds. The most spectacular acts followed, with Cody on horseback, using a Winchester to shoot composition balls in a number of ways, including hitting a ball thrown in the air while he rode past it at full gallop. After he had astounded the crowd with his skill with a Winchester, he finished by shooting the balls with his Colt's army revolver. [33]

There followed another act that remained a standard: the thrilling Attack upon the Deadwood Stage. This act later fascinated kings and princes. Richmond introduced driver John Highby; John Hancock beside him; Broncho Bill, the outrider; Con Groner on top of the coach. The passengers were drawn from the audience. Richmond told Highby that he had "entrusted you with valuable lives and property. Should you meet with Indians, or other dangers, en route, put on the whip, and if possible, save the lives of your passengers. If you are all ready, go!" Go it did, until suddenly a tremendous yell was heard and in galloped Indians, shouting and shooting.

The driver lashed his horses to a gallop. Somehow the driver stayed alive until at last Buffalo Bill and other horsemen appeared and charged the Indians. A tremendous battle broke out, but the Indians were driven away, and the adventure ended with "a blaze of Grecian fire from the interior of the coach in a realistic manner peculiar to the original genius of the West." [34]

There was a quieter spell, with Sioux boys racing bareback ponies and cowboys racing on Mexican thoroughbreds or mules. Then the Pawnee and Wichitas performed a number of ceremonies. The dancing, alas, was not always taken seriously by the white crowds. More to their taste no doubt was Mustang Jack, a jumper who leapt over horses and burros. Cowboys and vaqueros then went through their paces, including roping and tying Texas steers, before the sixteenth spot on the bill, the riding of an elk by Master Voter Hall, "a Feejee Indian from Africa," in reality a black American cowboy. [35]

The last act was the Attack on a Settler's Cabin, with John Nelson as the settler who comes home to enjoy his supper. Indians approach the cabin stealthily, one watching while the other steals Nelson's horse. Then the hunter's son sees the thief and fires. Out comes Nelson to find a whole band of Indians bearing down on the cabin. Enter cowboys at the gallop, and a running fight on horseback ensues, "with enough firing of pistols in it to make the small boy howl with delight,

men shot from their saddles and riderless steeds dashing around, the cowboys won their victory and the cabin was saved." Once more Buffalo Bill had come in the nick of time.

After that it merely remained for the entire cast to gather in front of the grand-stand. Cody bade the onlookers farewell and dismissed his cast. Then Richmond invited all to visit the troupe's camp be-fore they went home. This was a superb piece of public relations and was to be a huge success wherever Cody performed. [36]

The 1885 Wild West played in more than forty cities in the United States and Canada. It was a colossal success artis-tically and financially, and for a part of it there was a unique attraction, Sitting Bull himself. His reaction to Annie

JOHN *Y. Nelson and family photographed by Napoleon Sarony at Staten Island in 1886. Less than a year later he and his fam- ily were presented to Queen Victoria. (Courtesy Denver Public Library, Western Collection)*

Oakley's shooting has been noted, and when Major Burke was doing his best to sign up the great Indian, a photograph of Annie did the trick. He had not been treated well in his previous show, but now Burke was able to promise—after Sitting Bull saw Annie's photograph in Burke's tent—that he would see her every day. On June 6 he signed his con- tract, which involved a four-month stay with the show at $50 a week, two weeks' pay in advance, a $125 bonus, and the concession to sell photographs and auto- graphs of himself. Five other warriors signed up, along with three women and an interpreter. In the United States, Sit- ting Bull was liable to be booed when he appeared in the arena, though not in

Canada, where the crowds cheered him and government and other officials honored him. A few years earlier, because of a food shortage on the Plains and the fear of warfare between the Sioux and Blackfeet, it had been the duty of the North-West Mounted Police to get him back into the United States, but he himself was not regarded as an enemy. Now he was hailed by Canadian crowds.[37]

Happily, we know much about Sitting Bull's tour—how he liked attention and being introduced to people, how he was amazed at the poverty he saw, and how he gave money to various poor people. Upon meeting General Carr, Sitting Bull said, "The White people are so many that if every Indian in the West killed one every step they took, the dead would not be missed among you. I go back and tell my people what I have seen. They will never go on the war-path again." After his season he went home with a gray trick horse, a present from Cody. Cody also gave him a white sombrero, which one of his family once wore. Sitting Bull was furious. His friend "Long Hair" had given it to him. In view of what would soon happen, the story is poignant.[38]

The 1885 season ended at Columbus, Ohio, with a profit of $100,000. At last the Wild West had had a triumph. Cody, however, made a brief return to the stage with Buck Taylor in a piece called *The Prairie Waif*, in February 1886, before going back home to plan the next season. Cody and Salsbury were now in business. The stage could soon be forgotten. International fame was to be the destiny of the Wild West.

Cody had spent Christmas in North Platte. Show business featured in the town's life; Lloyd's Opera House, recently built, played host to "the celebrated Milan Opera Company" performing Bellini's *La Sonnambula* at the grand opening. Later in the season, the local hero himself starred in *The Prairie Waif*, which had been written for him in 1880 by John Stevens and described at the time as having "many startling tableaux," but "little of the 'blood and thunder' that characterized the Bowery drama of the past."[39]

The Wild West was now to enjoy a long engagement—six months—in one place, Erastina on Staten Island, named for the founder of the resort, Erastus Wiman. During the period on Staten Island, Cody engaged a newcomer who was to rival Annie Oakley. Lillian Smith, a fifteen-year-old from Coleville, Mono County, California, was soon dubbed "The California Girl." Lillian could hit a plate thirty times in fifteen seconds (presumably with a pair of lever-action Winchester rifles); break ten balls hung from strings and swinging around a pole; and fire four times after a glass ball had been thrown into the air, breaking it with the final shot. She had, it was claimed, started riding as an infant and shooting at age seven, eventually bagging forty mallard and redhead ducks in a day. Her first attempt at shooting at glass balls resulted in 323 successive shots without a miss. With a .22 caliber Ballard No. 3 Gallery

Rifle she broke 495 balls out of 500.[40]

Lillian accompanied Cody to North Platte and appeared in *The Prairie Waif*, where her shooting skill prompted one local editor to call her "the best shot in the world." He told his readers that her shooting bordered on the marvelous. Lillian broke twenty glass balls in twenty-four seconds with a Winchester, and twenty balls with a single-loading rifle [the Ballard?] in fifty-four seconds. "This is as fast as an ordinary gunman can shoot his piece, to say nothing of taking aim at a fast moving target. A beautiful feat was breaking two balls with one shot as the balls swung past each other in the air." Historians may long debate over which of the two girls was superior, but Lillian lacked Annie's star quality.[41]

The Wild West was now strong in the shooting department. Not only did Johnny Baker, coached by Annie, almost but not quite equal her prowess, but Seth Clover, using marbles as his targets, made a great impression. Cody was the practical all-round shot that the program stated he was, although in later years some claimed that he had faked many of his feats by using "bird shot" instead of ball ammunition. For example, Johnny Baker stated that around 1900 Buffalo Bill used a smooth-bore .44 caliber Winchester Model 1873 rifle, firing shells one-and-an-eighth inches long, loaded with twenty grains of black powder and a half ounce of no. 7½ chilled shot. This load was carefully worked out, for it enabled a shooter to hit moving targets or station-

LILLIAN Smith ca. 1886. She was recruited by Cody in California when she was fourteen. A local editor called her the best shot in the world. Lillian went to England in 1887. The Illustrated London News *pictured her being introduced to Queen Victoria. She did not remain with the Wild West for long, however, and later became Wenona, daughter of "Crazy Snake, a fighting chief of the Sioux," complete with darkened face, "the Indians holding her in awe and fear." (Yost,* Buffalo Bill, *167; Paul Fees to Robin May, November 11, 1986, citing Frederic T. Cummins's Indian Congress, Pan-American Exposition, Buffalo, N.Y., 1901.) (Courtesy Buffalo Bill Historical Center)*

ary ones twenty yards away with a two-inch pattern that was about the diameter of the resin "glass" balls that Cody and other marksmen and women regularly shot out of the air. Whether Cody ever owned and used smooth-bore pistols is a moot point, but Gordon W. Lillie, alias "Pawnee Bill," certainly did. The barrels on his .44 caliber Colt "Frontier Model" single-action revolvers were also slightly choked to concentrate the "bird shot" in the shells. The pistols were a gift from the Colt Company in 1891.[42]

Appearing in New York guaranteed a steady stream of celebrities. One, the great English actor Henry Irving, later the first actor-knight, was so thrilled by the Wild West that he later helped spread the word in London. Mark Twain not only loved the Wild West but urged that

it be taken to England so that the English could see a "purely and distinctive American" show. It was also, of course, a native American show, with the Indians in New York headed by American Horse the younger.[43]

Evening performances were introduced, at first with unfortunate results; gas flares, red fires to highlight the Indian scenes—the stagecoach attack and the dances—hardly helped the shooting sequences. A member of the staff suggested soaking cotton wads in alcohol, which were then glued on the clay pigeons. The flares were lit seconds before the traps were sprung. Unfortunately, sometimes the pigeon and the light parted company. One night both Annie and Cody missed ten times in succession. The back-lot genius had secured the lights to the clay pigeons with what then served as adhesive tape—court plaster! On this occasion, however, it was plastered on indeed. The shot did go through, but the pigeons survived intact.[44]

The Wild West had by now completely recovered the losses it had sustained at New Orleans—a single July week had brought in almost two hundred thousand patrons—so it was decided to take over Madison Square Garden for the winter. The director, Louis E. Cook, believed that "biggest is best" when it came to scenery. The lucky recipients of his imagination were Steel Mackaye, another big thinker and the author of *The Drama of Civilization*; Matt Morgan, the designer; and Nelse Waldron, who was responsible for the first double or moving stage seen in a theater. The roof literally had to be raised to contain the wonders below; twenty-five feet were added. A high spot was most of Deadwood reproduced for all to see—until the great moment came for a cyclone to destroy it. Realism was enhanced by one hundred bags of dried leaves, which blew over the vast stage.[45]

This was great showmanship, but something even better and certainly more important was in the offing. Eighteen eighty-seven was Queen Victoria's Golden Jubilee year, a matter of enormous significance to Britain and the Empire, which was now approaching its zenith. One of the innumerable planned events was an "Exhibition of the Arts, Industries, Manufactures, Products and Resources of the United States," an American enterprise that would indeed be called the American Exhibition. The organizers offered the Wild West the opportunity to perform for six months in London as an adjunct of the exhibition and to receive a percentage of the profits. The offer was accepted.[46]

Thus Buffalo Bill Cody made the most momentous decision of his life. It transported him from local to international fame and turned him into a living legend. On February 26, 1887, his forty-first birthday, the Wild West was incorporated, Cody and Salsbury each holding thirty-five shares with the remaining thirty going to three of their friends, William Guthrie, Frank C. Maeder (the brother of Fred Maeder, who wrote the

first Buffalo Bill melodrama), and
Milton E. Milner. John Burke went
ahead to London, but before going he so-
licited suitably glowing letters from leading army officers who knew Cody. Letters
from Sherman, Sheridan, Crook, Miles,
Carr, and others praised Cody and his
Wild West and recalled his good service
in the field. Governor Thayer's letter
dwelt on Cody's spell as "aide-de-camp of
my staff with the rank of colonel," a
"very ordinary sunburst title," as Don
Russell called it, but a useful one in high
company. It was hardly surprising that,
having been given a jewelled sword by
army officers, he became "Colonel Cody"
from that time onwards. Meanwhile, a
new contingent of Indians had been engaged: Sioux, Cheyenne, Kiowas, and
Pawnees, the most notable being the
Sioux Red Shirt. Handsome, dignified,
and witty, he had recently quelled a tribal
dispute involving a pretender to chief-
tainship, in which he marched straight
into the rebel camp with just two braves
and shot the pretender dead. He proved
as good a diplomat and leader on a remarkable adventure abroad as he was a
warrior.[47]

The *State of Nebraska* was the happy
choice of ship. Because of dire prophecies
of what would happen if they went on
water, prophecies that seemed reasonable
enough when the company was stricken
with seasickness, the Indians were reluctant to board the ship. The ship sailed
away on March 31 amid scenes of tremendous enthusiasm. The cowboy band

played "The Girl I Left Behind Me," as
Cody and Salsbury looked at the scene
below. Aboard were 83 saloon passengers,
38 steerage passengers, and 97 Indians—
more than 200 as Cody had promised—
along with 180 horses, 18 buffalo, 10 elk,
10 mules, 5 wild Texas steers, 4 donkeys,
and 2 deer. Bears may have also been
aboard. Annie Oakley is known not to
have been seasick in a severe storm that
hit the ship and continued for two days.
Cody and the rest were less fortunate.
The Indians sang their death songs as an
ailing Cody tried to make them believe
the condition would not last. After forty-
eight hours the storm stopped. A dam-
aged rudder added to the difficulties, but
at last they reached British waters.[48]

Timing, in show business as in life, is a
vital ingredient of success. The arrival of
Buffalo Bill's Wild West in England in
1887 was particularly well timed, though
for reasons not directly connected with
it. Twenty-two years had passed since the
strained relations of the Civil War period,
during which most of the ruling class had
favored the South. Many of the working
class, most notably the cotton workers of
Lancashire, whose livelihood had been
threatened by the Union's blockade of
Southern ports, sympathized with the
North for moral reasons. Few had the
vote, but they had a notable champion in
the Radical politician, John Bright, Lincoln's most active British supporter. In
the years that followed the war, relations
steadily warmed. The last obstacle to
close friendship was banished when the

British government made reparations for the depradations of the Confederate raider *Alabama,* which had been built in Britain (it cost the British government $15.5 million in gold, but in return the Americans agreed to ban privateers).[49]

The new warmth showed itself in a number of ways, not least in the growth of "Anglo-Saxonism" on both sides of the Atlantic. It did not matter that, like many Americans, many Britons were of Celtic descent, to say nothing of those descended from other European peoples. "Blood ties" were what counted. Henry James wrote his brother: "I can't look at the English-speaking world . . . save as a big Anglo-Saxon total," while a scholar named Hosmer wrote in 1890 what many were feeling—that America was losing her Anglo-Saxon character by "receiving all comers." Perhaps Commodore Josiah Tattnall put it best when asked why he had helped a British squadron bombard Korean batteries on shore in 1859. He stated bluntly, "Blood is thicker than water."[50]

With deepening friendship and a desire by some at least for a true reunion, it was hardly surprising that Cody, wherever his ancestors came from, had an especially strong welcome in England, for he was a stunning example of the Anglo-American race—and a hero to boot. The zeitgeist, the climate of opinion, was on his side; he arrived just as Queen Victoria was coming out of a retirement that dated back to her widowhood in 1861, about to celebrate her Golden Jubilee.

NOTES

1 Irving Wallace, *The Fabulous Showman* (London, 1960), 96–98; *Junction City Weekly Union,* September 5, 1868; *Daily Missouri Republican,* September 4 and 6, 1868; *Daily Illinois State Journal,* September 1, 5, and 10, 1868.

2 Nate (Nathan) Salsbury, "The Origin of the Wild West Show," *Colorado Magazine* 32, no. 3 (July 1955): 205–208.

3 Raymond W. Thorp, *Spirit Gun of the West: The Story of Doc. W. F. Carver* (Glendale, Calif., 1957), 19–20.

4 Diary of Ena Palmer Raymond, The Ena Palmer Raymond Ballentine McLeary Papers, Nebraska State Historical Society.

5 The late Paul D. Riley to Joseph G. Rosa, March 28, 1971; see also Thorp, *Doc. W. F. Carver.*

6 Agnes Wright Spring, *The Cheyenne and Black Hills Stage and Express Routes* (Glendale, Calif., 1949), 359.

7 *Omaha Daily Herald,* May 13 and 20, 1883.

8 Glenn Shirley, *Pawnee Bill: A Biography of Major Gordon W. Lillie* (Albuquerque, 1958), 102–103.

9 Don Russell, *The Lives and Legends of Buffalo Bill* (Norman, Okla., 1960; hereafter cited as Russell, *Lives*), 299.

10 Ibid., 299–300; Charles R. Nordin, "Dr. W. F. Carver, 'Evil Spirit of the Plains,'" *Nebraska History Magazine* 10, no. 4 (October–December 1927): 344–351.

11 Nate Salsbury, "The Origin of the Wild West Show," 207–208; Russell, *Lives,* 301.

12 Nate Salsbury, "The Origin of the Wild West Show," 204.

13 Ibid., 206–208.

14 Russell, *Lives,* 302–303.

15 Gene Fowler, *Timberline: A Story of Bonfils and Tammen* (New York, 1933), 46–48; Dexter W. Fellows and Andrew A. Freeman, *This Way to the Big Show* (New York, 1936), 90–92.

16 Charles Zurhorst, *The First Cowboy* (New York, 1973), 10–11; William Savage, Jr., ed., *Cowboy Life* (Norman, Okla., 1975), Introduction.

17 Russell, *Lives,* 308–309; Botkin, *Treasury,* 156.

18 W. F. Cody, *Story of the Wild West and Camp-Fire Chats* (Philadelphia, 1888; hereafter cited as Cody, *Story*),

698–699; Richard J. Walsh with Milton S. Salsbury, *The Making of Buffalo Bill* (Indianapolis, 1928; hereafter cited as Walsh, *Buffalo Bill*), 240–241; Sarah Blackstone, *Buckskins, Bullets, and Business* (Westport, Conn., 1986), 16–17.

19 Cody, *Story,* 698–699.

20 Nellie Snyder Yost, *Buffalo Bill: His Family, Friends, Failures, and Fortunes* (Chicago, 1979), 147; Walsh, *Buffalo Bill,* 243–244.

21 Russell, *Lives,* 311–313; see also Courtney Ryley Cooper, *Annie Oakley, Woman at Arms* (New York, 1927; hereafter cited as Cooper, *Annie Oakley*); Annie Fern Swartwout, *Missie* (Blanchester, Ohio, 1947); and Walter Havinghurst, *Annie Oakley of the Wild West* (New York, 1954).

22 Fellows and Freeman, *This Way to the Big Show,* 73.

23 Russell, *Lives,* 315–316; Stanley Vestal, *Sitting Bull: Champion of the Sioux,* 2nd ed. (Norman, Okla., 1957; hereafter cited as Vestal, *Sitting Bull*), 150; Swartwout, *Missie,* 70–71.

24 St. Louis *Daily Globe-Democrat,* May 15, 1885; William E. Deahl, Jr., "Buffalo Bill's Wild West Show, 1885," *Annals of Wyoming* 47, no. 3

(Fall 1975; hereafter cited as Deahl, "Buffalo Bill"): 144.

25 Deahl, "Buffalo Bill," 141; B. A. Botkin, ed., *A Treasury of American Folklore* (New York, 1944; hereafter cited as Botkin, *Treasury*), 150–155.

26 For a complete published copy of the typescript, see Botkin, *Treasury*, 150–156.

27 Deahl, "Buffalo Bill," 142.

28 Botkin, *Treasury*, 151; Deahl, "Buffalo Bill."

29 Burlington, Vermont, *Burlington Free Press and Times*, August 6, 1885; Botkin, *Treasury*, 151–152; Deahl, "Buffalo Bill," 143–144.

30 Botkin, *Treasury*, 152–53; Deahl, "Buffalo Bill," 145.

31 Botkin, *Treasury*, 153; Deahl, "Buffalo Bill," 145.

32 Ibid.

33 Botkin, *Treasury*, 154; Deahl, "Buffalo Bill," 145–147.

34 Botkin, *Treasury*, 154–155; Deahl, "Buffalo Bill," 147; Washington *Post*, June 23, 1885.

35 Botkin, *Treasury*, 155–156.

36 Ibid., 156; Deahl, "Buffalo Bill," 148–149; New Orleans *Daily Picayune*, December 24, 1884.

37 Russell, *Lives*, 316; John Peter Turner, *The North-West Mounted Police* (Ottawa, Ont., 1950), I, passim.

38 Vestal, *Sitting Bull*, 251; Cooper, *Annie Oakley*, 124; Russell, *Lives*, 316–317.

39 Yost, *Buffalo Bill*, 158–160.

40 Russell, *Lives*, 318; Norm Flayderman, *Flayderman's Guide to Antique American Firearms and Their Values*, 3rd. ed. (Northfield, Ill., 1983), 135.

41 Cody, *Story*, 699–700; Yost, *Buffalo Bill*, 167–168.

42 Harold F. Williamson, *Winchester: The Gun That Won the West* (New York, 1978), 188; John E. Parsons, *The Peacemaker and Its Rivals* (New York, 1950), 99.

43 Cody, *Story*, 713; Russell, *Lives*, 320–321.

44 Cooper, *Annie Oakley*, 141–151.

45 Russell, *Lives*, 322–323; Yost, *Buffalo Bill*, 179–180.

46 Cody, *Story,* 700.

47 Russell, *Lives,* 324–327; Cody, *Story,* 701–702.

48 Russell, *Lives,* 327.

49 Samuel Eliot Morison, Henry Steele Commager, and William E. Leuchtenburg, *The Growth of the American Republic,* I (London, 1980), 625, 647, 649, 690.

50 J. C. Furnas, *The Americans: A Social History of the United States, 1587–1914* (London, 1969), 605–613.

3

THE CONQUEST OF ENGLAND

Having lost a single horse on the transatlantic crossing—quite a feat considering the storm that had hit the *State of Nebraska* on the seventh day out from New York—the glamorous invaders sailed into the Thames Estuary on April 14. They cast anchor off Gravesend in Kent on the sixteenth. Considering the wildlife about to be disembarked, and the havoc that the recent outbreaks of rinderpest and foot-and-mouth disease had caused, the authorities could not have been more cooperative. The period of quarantine was kept to a minimum of a few days.[1]

One matter, however, did stir the authorities to action. When thousands of rounds of live ammunition were found on board, customs officers promptly confiscated them. In their place the authorities at Woolwich Arsenal supplied specially loaded blanks for arena use (the exceptions being the underloaded ammunition used by Cody and other sharpshooters), and the authorities also made arrangements to allow the arsenal of weapons to be imported without first entering customs bond. To maintain the weapons, Buffalo Bill engaged the services of Colt's London agent, Frederick von Oppen, whose descendants still prize signed photographs of Cody, Annie Oakley, and other show celebrities. Several times in later visits von Oppen's successor, James Goodbody, came to Cody's rescue when weapons needed repairing in a hurry.[2]

Meanwhile, Cody had plenty to think about as he gazed at the approach to the

BUFFALO *Bill as he looked when he arrived in England in 1887. This pose, particularly the turned-up sombrero, typifies the Buffalo Bill legend. The original illustration is a Woodburytype, which was popular at the time. The invention of Walter Woodbury of England in 1866, the type was processed from a lead block, which was brought, under great pressure, into contact with a hardened relief image made from gelatin and prepared photographically. The inked block was then pressed onto dampened paper. Once dry, the image was prepared for insertion into a book or copied for sale to the public. It was not a photograph in the true sense, but it appeared to be one. (Courtesy Colin Crocker)*

busiest port in the world. He considered the reality, "all of us combined in an expedition to prove to the center of old world civilization that the vast region of the United States was finally and effectively settled by the English-speaking race." His ruminations were interrupted by the approach of a tug flying the American flag. Handkerchiefs were waved wildly, and the travelers answered with shouts and cheers. "The Star-Spangled Banner" was played aboard the tug and was answered by the strains of "Yankee Doodle" played by the cowboy band. In the tug, led by Lord Ronald Gower, were the directors of the American Exhibition. John Burke was with them, along with many press representatives. Cody went ashore and was given a hearty welcome in the town where Pocahontas lies buried.[3]

After a ceremony of welcome had

taken place ashore, Cody and an advance guard of workers set off for the exhibition grounds at Earl's Court in West London, first by train to Victoria Station, then by underground railway to West Kensington. It was an exciting journey for Cody, as he later related, and at the end of it there was a "hearty repast" with enough strong drink to give the hero of the hour a considerable respect for the British as drinkers. Work began at once, with hundreds starting to prepare everything from grandstand to stables. Lights and bonfires helped the workers to fence the arena, build stands, and so on. The object was to allow forty thousand people into each performance. The only hold-ups occurred when British workers could not stop staring at Buffalo Bill. He retired from view.[4]

The slowness of the British workers was remarked on, but, slow or not, they were presumably not used to show business conditions. The Wild West's efficiency at setting up the show and dismantling it is legendary, but British show and circus folk were no slouches either.[5]

In fact, it was now time for Cody to return to the *State of Nebraska* for the journey up the Thames the following day. He set off by hansom cab and enjoyed a ride through the West End, finishing up at the Hotel Metropole on Northumberland Avenue. The hotel was full of his countrymen, who gave him a great welcome. He managed at last to get to bed and at dawn headed for Gravesend. The ship steamed up on the morning tide through the Port of London. Getting

THIS *famous full-length photograph of Buffalo Bill has been reproduced many times and variously dated. The original was made in 1887, possibly by Elliott & Fry, who made several plates of Cody similarly garbed. (Courtesy Buffalo Bill Historical Center)*

through customs was a mere formality that day, and soon three trains were carrying humans, beasts, and gear to West London. By four o'clock in the afternoon the horses were stabled, tents were sprouting, and the camp's cooks were hard at work. As Cody later described it, a canvas city had sprung up in the heart of West London. Then the flag was raised, the national anthem was played, and the thousands lining the walls and staring down from houses started cheering. The band played on. The dining room tents were not yet open; the crowds could enjoy watching the Americans eating at tables in the open air. By nine o'clock the camp was virtually finished, and the excited visitors settled down to sleep on English soil.[6]

The speed of the operation—the "set-up" in theatrical parlance—was a talking point among Londoners, just as the cold April showers would be a topic of morbid interest among westerners over the next few days. There was a stream of notables to the camp, one of the most welcome to Cody being the great actor Henry Irving, who, as we have noted, became Sir Henry Irving, the first theatrical knight. He had seen the Wild West at Staten Island and had written about it most

warmly in the theatrical paper the *Era.*
He noted a crucial difference between it
and a play: "However well it is re-
hearsed . . . it is impossible to avoid a
considerable share of the impromptu and
the unforeseen. For you may rehearse
with buffaloes as much as you like, but
no-one can say in what manner they will
stampede when they are suddenly turned
loose in the open." He predicted that the
show would take the town by storm.[7]

The *Daily Telegraph,* then the nation's
best-selling national newspaper, gave a
long description of the enterprise and the
American Exhibition in general on April
21. The writer had no doubts about
which would be the more popular and,
better still, got his facts right:

> However, undoubtedly the chief at-
> traction of this sample fragment of a
> vast continent that is to be anchored,
> or, as they say, "located," in our midst
> will be "Buffalo Bill's Wild West Ex-
> hibition." This peculiar and antique
> show, which won such enthusiastic ad-
> miration from Mr. Irving in America,
> is not acting or imitation of Western
> life, but an exact reproduction of the
> scenes of fierce frontier life vividly il-
> lustrated by the real people. Indian
> life, cowboy life, Indian fighting, the
> lasooing and breaking-in of wild
> horses, feats of strength, border ath-
> letic games, will be shown by a troupe
> that numbers over 200 Indians and
> cowboys.

THESE *magnificent thigh boots were made
for Cody by J. Neary of North Platte especially for his appearance in England. (Courtesy Buffalo Bill Historical Center)*

THIS *panoramic view of the cast of the Wild West was made in England ca. May– June 1887. Clearly visible is Buffalo Bill, and to his left (in top hat) is Nate Salsbury. To Cody's right is Buck Taylor (complete with crutches; Taylor had broken his leg some weeks before), and seated are Major John Burke and Johnny Baker. To Cody's rear right is Annie Oakley, and to the right of John Y. Nelson at the rear, Sergeant Bates grasps the Stars and Stripes. (Courtesy Buffalo Bill Historical Center)*

The writer then called Cody "this American Achilles of the cowboy Iliad."[8]

The *Times,* now as friendly to America as it had once been hostile, wrote of the exhibition as a whole at enormous length on April 27. The paper thanked "our American cousins" for "planting in our midst the biggest pleasure resort this country ever saw." This was no exaggeration, for it covered twenty-three acres. The main gallery was more than twelve hundred feet long, with three underground stations serving the site. There were great avenues named for famous Americans, and the whole was crammed with the "manufactures, products," etc., that were no less exotic than Red Indians, Annie Oakley, and the handsome star of the show. Red Shirt received his first *Times* review in this feature. The critic noted that he and the other Indians had been to see Irving's production of Goethe's *Faust* at the Lyceum Theater and had been "greatly scared at its horror" as they—and the cowboys—watched the proceedings from a number of boxes. The show seems to have been a lively version of Goethe's masterpiece, and the exotic visitors must have made it livelier. There were plenty of scenic effects, and

Irving was in form as Mephistopheles. (His grandson called it a histrionic romp, and it triumphed in New York the following year.) Red Shirt was called upon for his opinion and admirably summed it up as a big dream. Also much enjoyed by the company was a trip to Drury Lane Theatre to see the dog and monkey exhibition that was currently occupying the boards of the famous theater.[9]

The interest of theater people helped build up publicity for the coming show. Irving's enthusiasm has been noted, but another point must be stressed. Even more than today, the Anglo-American stage was a cousinly affair, indeed a family one in some cases. The Booths, the Drews, and the Barrymores were either of British descent or British-born, and this was an asset. So was the excited patronage of the aristocracy, and not simply those who had met Cody in the West. Besides, Cody was, to use a phrase that has only recently fallen into disuse in Britain, so clearly one of "nature's gentlemen."[10]

Most Americans in London seem to have joined in the welcome, but there were those who resented their country's being represented by a group of westerners, white and red. The poet James Russell Lowell, who had been American minister in London from 1880 to 1885, now took a swipe at Britons and Americans alike when he wrote: "I think the true key to this eagerness for lions—even the poodle sort—is the dullness of the average English mind."[11]

The hero of the hour was getting so many invitations that even his remarkable stamina was taxed. The most famous clubs opened their doors to him—he first met the Prince of Wales at the Reform—and "all that is great in literary, artistic and histrionic London," he noted, was opened to him.[12]

On April 25, the Grand Old Man (G.O.M.) of British politics, William Ewart Gladstone, currently leader of the opposition in Parliament, came to the camp at Earl's Court. The great and formidable statesman and orator was with Thomas Waller, the consul general of the United States in London, and they were given a glimpse of what the Wild West would be like when it opened on May 9. Gladstone met Red Shirt, as grand a figure as the G.O.M. himself. (His enemies had christened him the M.O.G.—murderer of Gordon—in 1885, blaming him for the death of General Gordon at Khartoum.) At lunch Gladstone toasted Cody and his show, and Waller, too, spoke warmly. Cody began to get an inkling of just what a part he was to play in cementing Anglo-American relations.

On May 5, four days before the official opening, a crucial event took place. Cody had invited the Prince of Wales to a special performance, a preview of the show. Later, he would wonder how he had ever managed to get everything ready on time, not only because of the work to be done, but because of the constant invitations he had. Also his Indians—from Pine Ridge—were new to the show, and

THE *original Deadwood Stage against an arena backdrop, London, 1887. John Nelson and two of his children are seated on top of the coach. Major John Burke is standing on* the lead chassis. *Standing in front are Johnny Baker and Buffalo Bill, and lounging against the rear wheel is the giant figure of Buck Taylor. (Courtesy Scout's Rest Ranch)*

so were a hundred of his Texas ponies. Worse still, diabolical weather had made the ground something of a quagmire, which was not improved by having timber dragged across it. However, it was a chance of a major rehearsal, albeit in company that had to be impressed. [13]

The royal box was "handsomely rigged out" for the occasion with the Union flag and the Stars and Stripes, and a notable party appeared to sit in it. Along with the prince and princess and their three daughters, there were British, German, and French aristocrats and their attendants. Cody, Salsbury, and Burke met them all. Cody described the prince as

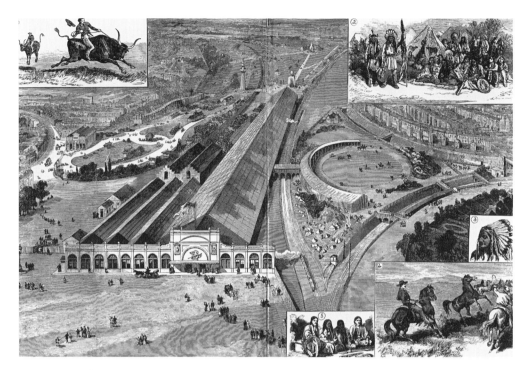

THIS *magnificent panoramic drawing appeared in the* Illustrated London News *of April 16, 1887. Buffalo Bill buffs should not try to find evidence of these marvels—the area has been totally changed. (From the collection of Robin May)*

the *beau idéal* of a plain-spoken, pleasant, kindly gentleman who took universal homage as a matter of course but never acted as if he would exact it. He found less pride in the prince than in third-rate civic officials everywhere. The prince would be a good friend to and ambassador for Cody down the years.[14]

In fact, Cody was having the afternoon equivalent of first-night nerves, made worse by the state of the ground. Burke and Frank Richmond were left in the box as comperes, and Cody walked away. He need not have worried. The prince signaled that he and his party were ready and, as Cody described it, "the Indians, yelling like fiends, galloped out from their ambuscade and swept round the enclosure like a whirlwind. The effect was instantaneous and electric. The prince rose from his seat and leaned eagerly over the front of the box, and the whole party thrilled at the spectacle. 'Cody,' I said to myself, 'you have fetched 'em!'"[15]

He had indeed, for everything went

splendidly, not least the moment when Lillian Smith and Annie Oakley shook Princess Alexandra's proferred hand instead of kissing it. Annie's own account has her showing a most diplomatic tact. Having heard that women tried to flirt with the prince, whose roving eye has been a godsend to the entertainment industry down the years, she ignored his hand when it came over the front of the box and extended hers to the lovely princess, who took it gently and said, "What a wonderful little girl!" The prince had no objection and now shook her hand warmly, remarking as she started to go, "What a pity there are not more women in the world like that little one." Lillian Smith also shook hands. It is a matter of record that this royal preview lasted over an hour and a half and that the prince stood for the greater part of it.[16]

Now it was time for a visit to the camp. The prince met Red Shirt and told him how much he had enjoyed what he had seen, while the princess welcomed him to England. "Tell the Great Chief's wife that it gladdens my heart to hear her words of welcome," said the dignified Sioux. The prince asked him if he found the weather cold. "Not as cold as Dakota!" was the reply. John Nelson and his family, especially his youngest child, made a great hit with the royal party. The prince headed for Cody's headquarters tent, where he was greatly taken by the gold-mounted sword given Cody by his high-ranking army friends. Then, despite the churned-up mud, the prince asked to

see the stables. This was a surprise, but Cody's "equine arrangements" were strictly military, and the visit was yet another success, even more so because the prince demanded to know the life story of the twenty-year-old Old Charlie, Cody's beloved horse. Finally, at seven o'clock the visitors departed, with the prince giving the contents of his cigar case to Red Shirt. Cody, Burke, and Salsbury relaxed and congratulated each other on an auspicious start.[17]

News reached Nebraska of these triumphs, which delighted all but Codyphobes, notably the *Omaha World.* Meanwhile, Londoners were catching Codymania, an odd offshoot being a resurgence of interest in the novels of James Fenimore Cooper. Or was it so odd? Although the novels might have been about the eastern forests a century earlier, they were genuinely American. Because they had Indians and frontiersmen in them, they sold by thousands. Cody was delighted with the intense interest in his country and its people. Later he wrote, "I am proud of my small share in this desirable state of things, which will be a source of comfort to me to my dying day."[18]

The weather relented just in time for the grand opening on May 9. Admission for that performance was one pound, then the equivalent of about five dollars. Inflation makes a mockery of such figures, but it might help to note that a British working man with a small family in a city could live on just over one pound a week

ALEXANDRA, *Princess of Wales, photographed by George E. Hansen of Copenhagen ca. 1867. Twenty years later she was even more enthusiastic about the Wild West than was the rest of the royal family. She not only rode in the Deadwood Stage but also watched a performance from the press box incognito as a member of the press—and her* cover was not blown. *(From the collection of Joseph G. Rosa)* ABOVE

RED *Shirt, an Oglala Sioux, was the leading Indian of the Wild West on its first trip to Britain and Europe. (Courtesy Smithsonian Institution, National Anthropological Archives)* RIGHT

CODY'S *admiration for Red Shirt led to this autographed portrait in 1888 of Buffalo Bill dressed in army uniform. (Courtesy Union Pacific Railroad Museum)*

at that time. For ordinary performances tickets ranged from one to four shillings: about twenty-five cents to one dollar. The *Times* stated that twenty-eight thousand people attended the opening. Between twenty thousand and forty thousand a day was to be the average attendance, with two performances a day. If the figures in the *Times* are correct, the stands must have been packed indeed.[19]

Cody claimed that the daily expenses of the show were $2,500, and that it cost him a great deal more to feed his troupe in England than it did in the United States. An "English laborer thinks he is lucky if he gets meat to eat once a week, while the American must have it two or three times a day. Fresh beef costs a shilling a pound over there, and when it comes to feeding such a large number of hungry Indians, whose principal article of food is meat, the expense is enormous."[20]

Not surprisingly, the opening performance was a triumph. The *Sporting Life* summed it up best: "It is new, it is brilliant, it will 'go'!" It was undoubtedly a social event. The same scribe noted that "the number of chariots waiting at the gates outnumbered those of Pharoah, and the phalanx of footmen constituted a small army." The *Times*'s editorial writer made some pertinent points. He noted

how the Wild West outshone the rest of the exhibition, and he took another swipe at Gladstone and his Irish policy, again mentioning that America also had its Irish problem. More importantly, he proclaimed: "A quarrel between Great Britain and America would be a calamity of so tremendous a kind that there is every excuse of declining to regard it as possible." Cody, so often denigrated then and now, played his part in making such a calamity impossible.[21]

As a sea of good to magnificent reviews followed the opening performance, so two rather offbeat ones will not come amiss to those jaded with raves. One reviewer, quoted by Cody in his account of the London appearances, was particularly taken with the bucking horses, the attack on the Deadwood Stage, Mustang Jack's leaps, Cody's shooting at the gallop, and also with Lillian Smith's shooting. Annie Oakley did not always steal the reviews. The same scribe advised that wigs, scalps, and carmine should be hired so that hair could be lifted realistically. Cody was genuinely shocked and wished the fellow could see the real thing.[22]

Another reviewer, this time in the *Illustrated London News*, mused over a trip he had made to the United States, where in an Atlanta bar he noticed two remarkable-looking men, finely dressed, complete with gold-topped canes and long flaxen hair and wide-brimmed hats. When he asked the bartender who they were, he was told that they claimed to be

Buffalo Bills. In his ignorance of western parlance he assumed that "Buffalo Bill-ism" might be a generic term for some occidental institution. Later, he became rapturous in his praise:

> All hail to the cow-boys, the "greasers," the Indians on ponies, the rescuers of the Deadwood stagecoach, with Lord Ronald Gower among the passengers! all honour to the American frontier girls who ride so fearlessly! Buffalo Bill's entertainment is assuredly the most remarkable ever seen in this country. It is to be hoped that the triumph of Buffalo Bill, his Indians and his cowboys, and his immense stock of "bronco" (not "broncho") horses will not make Barnum "feel bad," nor cause that patriarch of showmen to take a back seat.

The writer went on to note that even if the exhibition flagged, Buffalo Bill was strong enough to carry the whole show on his shoulders.[23]

There followed an even more important royal occasion than that of the Prince of Wales and his party. Queen Victoria had become virtually a recluse after the death of her husband, Prince Albert, in 1861. The prince's death affected both her own popularity and that of the monarchy. This changed in the late 1870s, with Prime Minister Benjamin Disraeli not only steering the British Empire towards its zenith but skillfully

AMONG the attractions that Londoners saw in 1887 was the bearded figure of Gabriel Dumont (between Annie Oakley and Lillian Smith). He had taken a prominent part in the Riel Rebellion in Canada in 1885 and fled to the United States afterwards. Such was Cody's power and prestige that no one queried the presence of a wanted man. Even his enemies respected him. (From the collection of Robin May)

bringing the queen out of the shadows and helping identify her with the nation's successes. Yet though she had been a keen theater- and opera-goer in her youth, now she "summoned" shows to Windsor and other palaces. All this would change in 1887, her Golden Jubilee year, and it is a matter of record that her first "show" outside her palaces for many years was the Wild West.[24]

The queen had "commanded" Cody and company to perform at Windsor, but he pointed out politely that the show was too big to take there. To everyone's surprise, and to the delight of Cody, the queen, therefore, agreed to come to see the Wild West at Earl's Court. She stipulated, however, that the show must last only an hour. Recovering quickly from this edict, all hands got down to work, including the setting up of a bright, beautiful, flower-covered royal box. Stage-fright was rampant.[25]

May 11 was the great day, even greater than anyone can have anticipated. A large and notable throng appeared with

the queen, including the Prince and Princess of Battenberg (parents of Lord Louis Mountbatten), and also a man who knew more about North American Indians than did most Britons. He was the Marquis of Lorne, an ex-governor general of Canada, who was married to the queen's daughter Louise.[26]

A stirring and historic episode followed. In public as in private life, gestures matter, and now Queen Victoria, granddaughter of George III, made a memorable one. At each performance a horseman came into the arena bearing the American flag, as Frank Richmond proclaimed it an emblem of peace and friendship. On this occasion the queen arose and bowed deeply to the Stars and Stripes. The rest of the party stood, the ladies bowing, the noblemen raising their hats, the military men saluting. The Americans gazed at the spectacle and, as Cody later described it, "there arose such a genuine heart-stirring American yell from our company as seemed to shake the sky." It was a magnificent moment. Cody's own comments contain the heart of the matter:

All present were constrained to feel that here was an outward and visible sign of the extinction of that mutual prejudice, amounting sometimes almost to race hatred, that had severed two nations from the times of Washington and George the Third to the present day. We felt that the hatchet

was buried at last and the Wild West had been at the funeral.[27]

Not surprisingly, the show went particularly well and, indeed, was given complete. It even ran over by a quarter of an hour. Then came the presentations. Cody was too modest to commit to paper what the queen said to him. Lillian Smith explained the mechanism of her Winchester rifle to the queen. Annie Oakley was introduced, along with a blushing Nate Salsbury. Red Shirt told the queen that he had come a long way to see her and felt glad, then turned and walked regally away. The last to be presented were two Indian women and their "papooses." Both children, one of them Bennie, the son of Bronco Bill Irving and his wife Ella, were petted by the queen—and so ended a most memorable occasion.[28]

When she got back to Windsor Castle, the queen confided the details of her adventure to her journal:

. . . to Earl's Court, where we saw a very extraordinary & interesting sight, a performance of "Buffalo Bill's Wild West." We sat in a box in a large semi circle. It is an amphitheatre with a large open space, all the seats being under cover. All the different people, wild, painted Red Indians from America, on their wild bare backed horses, of different tribes,—cow boys, Mexicans, &c., all came tearing round at

QUEEN *Victoria's historic and much-enjoyed visit to the Wild West on May 11, 1887, was recorded in the* Illustrated London News *on May 21. It is worth not-* *ing that the artist recorded Lillian Smith, not Annie Oakley, being introduced to the queen. (From the collection of Robin May)*

full speed, shrieking & screaming, which had the weirdest effect. An attack on a coach & on a ranch, with an immense deal of firing, was most exciting, so was the buffalo hunt, & the bucking ponies, that were almost impossible to sit. The cow boys, are fine looking people, but the painted Indians, with their feathers, & wild dress (very little of it) were rather alarming looking, & they have cruel faces. A young girl, who went through the "haute école," certainly sat the most marvellous plunges beautifully, sitting quite erect, & being completely master of her horse. There were 2 other girls, who shot with unvarying aim at glass balls. Col: Cody "Buffalo Bill," as he is

SIOUX *Indians against a backdrop at Earl's Court, London, photographed by Vandyk.*   *(Courtesy Scout's Rest Ranch)*

called, from having killed 3000 buffaloes, with his own hand, is a splendid man, handsome, & gentlemanlike in manner. He has had many encounters & hand to hand fights with the Red Indians. Their War Dance, to a wild drum & pipe, was quite fearful, with all their contorsions [sic] & shrieks, & they came so close. "Red Shirt" the Chief of the Sioux tribe, was presented to me & so were the squaws, with their papooses (children), who shook hands with me. Lorne had met me, & presented the different gentleman of the Executive Council. The performance ended, we drove straight to Paddington Station & returned to Windsor, getting there by ½ p[ast] 7.[29]

Eighteen months later, when he was interviewed by a reporter at Leavenworth

THE *Attack upon a Settler's Cabin, which was always popular with audiences. From a* *photograph by Vandyk. (Courtesy Scout's Rest Ranch)*

who was anxious to grip the hand that had "grasped Victoria's," Cody said that he had been more than satisfied both with the success of his show and with the treatment he had received in London. However, once the queen condescended to visit the Wild West, "the people considered it *the thing* to go to the show, and thousands were turned away from the enormous pavilions."[30]

Bronco Bill had ridden one of Cody's three Montana bucking horses at the Command Performance, a spectacular debut for the horse, which was promptly christened Jubilee. By the end of the sea-

son it was tame enough, but not yet. Cody swiftly dismissed suggestions that the bronco riding was fixed. Indeed, Buck Taylor had suffered a broken leg within two weeks of their arrival in England, and hardly a performance passed without some injury. "The Englishmen got so that if nobody was hurt during a performance they were disappointed, so when no one was hurt, I would instruct one of the boys to pretend to be injured, and they wouldn't know the difference." Asked if anyone in the audience had ever managed to ride one of the broncos, Cody said that only one man had managed to

ANOTHER *Vandyk photograph, this time depicting the rescue of the Deadwood Stage by Buffalo Bill and his cowboys. The colonel* *gallantly hands down one of the lady passengers. (Courtesy Scout's Rest Ranch)*

stay on more than thirty seconds. "He was a good rider, if not better, than any of my cowboys. He proved to be an Australian bronco breaker."[31]

Cody dispensed hospitality to a steady stream of distinguished visitors. He must have been pleased to be able to return his new friends' hospitable treatment. John Bright had the misfortune to trip and hurt his nose as he entered the welcome tent, but he was speedily looked after and able to go to his box seat, cheered by the audience who had heard of his misfor-

tune. The rubber mat at the door had caused his accident. Winston Churchill's father, Lord Randolph Churchill, laughingly leapt over the mat when he came to see Cody. His twelve-year-old son Winston, at school in Brighton, begged his American-born mother, Jennie, Lady Randolph Churchill, to let him come up for Buffalo Bill and the Jubilee as he had been promised. If not, he would never trust her promises again. Jennie, it will be remembered, was the daughter of Leonard W. Jerome, who had once

THE *Deadwood Stage at Earl's Court drawn by six mules (two of them are out of frame). The driver is Tom Duffey, who had once driven the coach between Cheyenne and* *Deadwood. John Nelson is seated at the rear. From an original Woodburytype. (Courtesy Colin Crocker)*

hunted with Cody and made him welcome when he first visited New York. Winston's pleas seem to have worked, for the next letters are not those of a boy who had missed Buffalo Bill![32]

Many Americans called on Cody, and he and Salsbury decided to throw a rib roast breakfast. The meal was cooked by the Indians, all of whom ate with the visitors, Red Shirt being among the speakers. Invitations for the afternoon's performance were offered to all.[33]

Cody's social life between performances has been the subject of much speculation—his detractors have asserted that he went about in an alcoholic haze among his aristocratic friends or dallied with ladies of his choice. However, the facts suggest otherwise. Like most of us, he tried to escape on weekends, and he would disappear to the Oatlands Park Hotel at Weybridge, Surrey, where he soon became a familiar sight. The place had a history going back to Henry VIII, but the hotel building was not constructed until 1856. Since Cody's time it has undergone many changes—it served as a military hospital in World War I— but despite modernization, the present owners think "Colonel Cody would still recognize it."[34]

Those Nebraskans who had little time

THE two most famous British statesmen of the day, William Ewart Gladstone (left) and Benjamin Disraeli, were turned into Indians by a Punch cartoonist in the May 7, 1887, issue. The caption is pun-packed (a feature of the period): "Red Shirt," Chief of the Seeyou-at-West Kensington Indians, receives a visit from "Grand Old White Collar," alias "Strong Will," Chief of the Opper Sishun Hinderuns. (From the collection of Robin May)

for Cody, and who resented his being chosen by the governor to be Nebraska's commissioner and representative at the Jubilee and the world's fair, had a bad summer. At this distance it sounds like sour grapes, made the sourer because Cody seemed to have everything—fame, fortune, the friendship of the royal family and the aristocracy and, indeed, of everyone he met. Not all can have been overwhelmed by the Wild West, but finding criticism of it in Britain is hard labor. It is fair to criticize Cody's conduct at times, but to this day there are those who like to characterize him as a "bum" or a "drunken bum." No Briton is known to have found him so. And the British welcomed the appearance of his daughter Arta, comparing her favorably with louder American ladies they had met.[35]

The queen asked for another command performance especially for her Jubilee guests. This took place on June 20, the day before the day of days. Naturally, London was packed with royalty and other distinguished visitors from home and abroad, and this was the queen's sensible idea of giving as many of them as possible a good time. Five kings and three crown princes were among the guests, and a famous ride in the Deadwood Stage took place, with Buffalo Bill at the reins. The kings of Belgium, Denmark, Greece, and Saxony, as well as the Prince of Wales, were inside. They were attacked by Indians and no doubt thoroughly enjoyed themselves. After the show, the

Prince of Wales said to Cody: "Colonel, you never held four kings like these before!" "I've held four kings," Cody replied, "but four kings and the Prince of Wales makes a royal flush, such as no man ever held before." The prince roared with laughter, then tried to explain the joke to the other royalty, no easy feat. America had given Britain poker in 1871 when General Robert C. Schenk was appointed American ambassador to Britain, and he taught the game to London society. Later, Cody would improve the story of the ride by changing his reply to the prince to "four kings and the Royal Joker." Also later, Princess Alexandra, the Princess of Wales, demanded a ride in the coach. Although her husband was somewhat anxious, the princess greatly enjoyed the ride.[36]

The only group of Britons which did not wholeheartedly welcome the Wild West was the circus fraternity, most notably George Sanger. He had some reason to resent the presence of the real thing, because he had been presenting a show of his own, *Scenes from Buffalo Bill.* He had several genuine buffalo, some alleged Indians, and a stagecoach that would not have survived on the plains. In fact, Sanger was a great showman, not to be judged by his western efforts. As soon as Cody arrived in Britain, Sanger made his *Scenes* a more prominent part of his circus than that show normally was. Later, in his otherwise admirable autobiography he gives the impression that his American

ARTA *Cody ca. 1883. She inherited her mother's eyes and Latin looks. In 1887, Arta joined Cody in England, where she was received into London society and had many admirers. Back in Nebraska, however, where some disgruntled Omahans resented Buffalo Bill's appointment as the state's commissioner and representative to Queen Victoria's Jubilee, ungallant remarks about how "stout" she was appeared in the* Herald. *But one of its rivals, the* Tribune, *was delighted to report that the British thought she was a credit to her country. (Courtesy Buffalo Bill Historical Center)*

rivals were second-raters. However, some fun was had by the public in the meantime.[37]

Before describing this, it must be admitted that unlike Sanger the music hall—vaudeville—fraternity in Britain did have some cause for complaint. None of them were lionized like Cody, and one of the stars of the "halls," a brilliant male impersonator named Vesta Tilley, sang a Jubilee song called "May Queen Victoria Reign," which was mainly a paean of praise but had two verses that were more than somewhat reproachful:

> She's seen the Yankee Buffaloes,
> The circus, too, from France,
> And may she reign until she gives
> The English show a chance.
> May Queen Victoria reign
> May she long with us remain
> Till Irving takes rank with a

> war-painted Yank,
> May good Queen Victoria reign.[38]

The French circus referred to was from the Hippodrome, Paris, and was performing near the Wild West at Olympia.

Sanger's Buffalo Bill *Scenes* had been featured in his show for about a year before the Americans arrived. Cody now set about, through his agents, "plastering over the bills of every rival show throughout the country," for others were eager to get into the act, but Sanger, "out of sheer cussedness," determined to keep his version of the Wild West on the program. This infuriated Cody, who sued Sanger, and the rivals met at the high court in London's Strand. Sanger recalled, "He went into the box, and I went into the box, and a very pretty display of contradictory statements resulted. After I had said what I had to say, I went off to Barnet, where my circus then was, to look after my business and await the result." This came in the middle of the afternoon performance when a telegram advised him that he had won the day, which was read to the audience "who cheered me heartily, and I promised to put the facts before them in a special bill."[39]

An examination of the *Times'* report of the case, however, discloses a very different result, one that was not to Sanger's credit. On August 12, 1887, before Mr. Justice Chitty, Sanger, through his counsel, Mr. Marten, Q.C., and Mr. Wood Hill, undertook not to use "Buffalo Bill" or "Wild West" in a manner that could be construed to mean that Cody was a member of his organization. On August 19, however, Cody received a letter from Sanger in which Sanger claimed that he would depict the "Wild West" in defiance of any order. In court on August 31 it was stated by the defense that the letter had not been written by Sanger—presumably it had been written by some other party with malicious intent—but it was admitted that the program was a true representation of what had been performed at various places in southern England.

The judge, Mr. Justice Kekewich, examined the program, which contained such blurbs as "Royal Olympia—Scenes from Buffalo Bill and the Far West" and "The mail on its perilous journey through the Wild West—attacked by Indians—the arrival of Buffalo Bill and the cowboys—great encounter—the Indians driven off—Buffalo Bill and the cowboys triumphant—escort of the mail!" The judge not surprisingly decided this was a direct infringement of Sanger's undertaking, and while he accepted the fact that Mr. Sanger may have been unaware of any breach, he nevertheless created the impression that Cody was a member of his organization and would appear. Giving leave to issue a writ of attachment against Mr. Sanger, he did, however, order that it be deferred for a week to give Sanger time to purge his contempt but pay the costs.

On September 7 Sanger's counsel pre-

"LORD" *George Sanger, Cody's English rival, ennobled himself to combat the latter's "Honorable." Fortunately, Queen Victoria was amused. The sketch is based on a carte-de-visite, ca. 1887. (From the collection of Joseph G. Rosa)*

sented the court with a specimen of the revised program that proved acceptable to the court. The judge ruled that he could use the words "Buffalo Bill" and "Wild West" but was to make clear that there was no connection with Colonel Cody. The revised program declared that

"George Sanger's Buffalo Bill" and his "Bully Boys"—evidently a dig at Cody's court action—had "no connection with any other person known as Buffalo Bill either in London or the provinces," and no one could now connect Cody with the performance.

Cody's counsel, however, declared that the change of wording was still insufficient because Sanger proposed to publish identical illustrations to those used by Cody—even to "Buffalo Bill in a blue shirt, riding to the rescue of the mail" and the "expression of horror on the driver's face." This was simply an evasion to which Mr. Justice Kekewich humorously remarked that such a ploy was what Lord Justice Brown had called "a pictorial lie."

In his summary, the judge stated that the program as it now stood was unobjectionable, but he warned Sanger that if he published identical material to that used by Colonel Cody, he did so at his own risk. In discharging the writ of attachment, the judge ordered Mr. Sanger to pay the costs of the application.[40]

Sanger, irritated by the "continual reiteration of the phrase 'The Honourable William Cody,'" declared: "If he is the Honourable William Cody, then I'm Lord George Sanger!" And such he became and in legend still is.[41]

It only remains to record that other British showmen started giving themselves titles, culminating with an acrobat who was famed for his fall head downwards at a rope's end almost to the ground, and who now called himself King Ohmy. According to Sanger's autobiography, Queen Victoria was amused by his claim to a title.[42]

Whatever rivals might have felt, nearly everyone else seems to have succumbed to the spell of the Wild West during the enchanted Jubilee summer. Yet the strain was beginning to tell on Cody and, like other Americans, he felt that the English climate did not suit him. Basically, the trouble was the sheer pace of the life he was leading. He reckoned he was occupied for eighteen hours out of twenty-four, and he never missed a performance. Between twenty and forty thousand people a day had every reason to be grateful to him. He even found time to plan an English colony in Nebraska consisting of one hundred worthy families. He arranged for it to be built on his property. The scheme foundered, however, as it was feared that local workers might be put out of a job.[43]

The last London performance came on the evening of October 31, 1887. The next day the *Times* showed how important the Wild West had been, not least for giving a boost to the more sober exhibition, which was visited by many who had attended the infinitely more glamorous show. On that last day there was a meeting of representative Englishmen and Americans for the setting up of a court of reparation between Great Britain and the United States. The *Times* noted the astonishment of some of Cody's compatriots that he had become the hero of the London season. The paper also praised his sheer energy and the way he had found time to go everywhere despite his daily engagements. It rejoiced in the fact that the close of his show had been selected as the moment to promote a great international movement. "The Thunderer," as some affectionately referred to the *Times*, then the most influential newspaper in the English-speaking world, was not given to exaggeration. Praise from such a source was praise indeed. It ended with the following:

> This association of the cause of international arbitration with the fortunes of the Wild West is not without its grotesque aspects. But it has a serious import, nevertheless. After all, the Americans and the English are of one stock. Nothing that is American comes altogether amiss to an Englishman. We are apt to think that American life is not picturesque. We have been shown one of its most picturesque aspects. It is true that "RED SHIRT" would be as unusual a phenomenon in Broadway as in Cheapside. But the Wild West, for all that[,] is racy of the American soil. We can easily imagine Wall Street for ourselves; we need to be shown the cow-boys of Colorado. Hence it is no paradox to say that COLONEL CODY has done his part in bringing America and England nearer together.⁴⁴

WHEN *the Wild West visited Birmingham following the London season, two of the company remained on special and spectacular duty. Broncho Charlie Miller and Marve Beardsley challenged two cyclists, the Englishman Richard Howell and a Philadelphian, W. M. Woodside, to a six-day race. It took place at the Agricultural Hall, Islington, London. The riders raced for eight hours a day. Thirty horses were used and were changed every hour. There was a prize of three hundred pounds, a splendid sum in 1887, and the riders won by two miles and two laps. It was close all along, with a pace of some twenty miles an hour, and it was a huge success with the public. Each of the riders covered 407 miles, the cyclist Woodside 422, and his colleague 389 miles. For a full account, see Gladys Shaw Erskine,* Broncho Charlie, A Saga of the Saddle: The Autobiography of Broncho Charlie Miller *(London, 1935), a vastly entertaining, if not always reliable, tale. The plate is from the* Illustrated London News, *November 12, 1887. (From the collection of Robin May)*

Annie Oakley and Frank Butler left the show at the end of the season. There seems no direct evidence that this was because of Cody's alleged jealousy of Annie Oakley's success. She was a star in her own right outside the show, notably her victory over Duke Michael of Russia in a match that Cody himself set up at the special request of the Prince of Wales. Oakley's rich social life culminated in an

invitation to shoot in Berlin at the Charlottenburg racecourse, an event patronized by the German crown prince. Though the exact reasons for her departure are not clear—and she would later return—it was a logical step for someone who would now be called a superstar, with her efficient and loving partner, Frank Butler.[45]

Meanwhile, the tour of Britain opened in Birmingham on November 5, a late opening for an open air show in Britain, even if British winters are never as cold as those in much of the United States. However, "Brummagen" folk, also known as "Brummies," gave the show a tremendous welcome. They saw it that much better on the fourteenth, when the electrical installation from Earl's Court was brought north, ten carbon arc lights totalling 150,000 candlepower. Fortunately, the next stop would see them under cover. This was in Manchester, the cotton capital, surrounded by other bustling towns which, with "Cottonopolis," held six million people. The Manchester racecourse at Salford was the site of the "largest theater ever seen in the world, heated by steam and illuminated by the electric light."[46]

While this marvel was being prepared, Cody and his daughter Arta had a short holiday in Italy, during which they checked the Colosseum in Rome as a possible site for the Wild West. It was unsuitable, however, though later, as will be seen, the bigger Roman arena at Verona

was used successfully. The Codys hastened back to Manchester to see how things were progressing.[47]

Next to the "largest theater ever seen" a building had been erected in March to hold the whole company's tents and tepees, also complete with electric lighting and steam heating. Colossal scenery depicting western scenes was painted, and, of course, stables were at hand. Ten thousand people could be packed in. The opening show took place on the afternoon of December 17, and by the end of it, Buffalo Bill and his show had conquered Cottonopolis. Cody endeared himself still more by promising local schools and charitable institutions that there would always be free places for young waifs on Wednesday afternoons, even if paying customers were turned away.[48]

The show's seven episodes began with Indians in the "primeval forest" dancing, using sign language, fighting, etc. It included a prairie fire threatening a wagon train, plus a stampede of wild animals, which was a tremendous spectacle. There was a scene on a cattle ranch featuring sharp-shooting Lillian Smith and Emma Hicock [sic], as Emma Robinson was billed, along with her title as Queen of the Saddle. Emma was the daughter of Agnes Lake Thatcher, who had married Wild Bill Hickok five months before his murder and was herself a prominent circus performer. Emma was also described as The Champion Equestrienne of the

A REMINDER *of how much livestock appeared in the Wild West, Samuel Carter's drawing depicting Buffalo Bill hunting his* namesake *appeared in the* Illustrated London News *on June 18, 1887. (From the collection of Robin May)*

World. Custer's Last Stand was refought, and the grand climax was a reenactment of Deadwood City's destruction by a cyclone, which had proved so successful at Madison Square Garden, but this time courtesy of the Blackman Air Propeller Company.[49]

Cody noted that in the North those leaders of the community he met were more like their equivalents in America, self-made men who had reached the top through effort, rather than through inherited wealth. As in London, the hospitality was overwhelming, not least from the local Freemasons, who greeted him as one of their own. The company organized a series of horse-racing and athletic meetings on the Manchester racetrack. Despite the weather, vast numbers attended. Homesickness was clearly growing, but it was offset by the goodwill of the northerners.[50]

EMMA *Lake Thatcher, the stepdaughter of Wild Bill Hickok, appeared with Cody in Europe in 1887–89 and was billed as Emma Hickok, "The Champion Equestrienne of the World." From a stereoscope copyrighted by Underwood & Underwood, Liverpool, England, in 1889. (From the collection of Joseph G. Rosa)*

The last indoor performance took place on April 30. Cody received a five-minute ovation and was almost buried in flowers. The next day fifty thousand turned out for a benefit performance given for him by "the racecourse people." The final entertainment was a race of ten miles between English thoroughbreds and American broncos. Tony Esquival rode the American mounts, and a rider named Latham, the British ones. The American won, primarily because he adopted the so-called "Pony Express Mount" by leaping from one mount to another while both animals were in motion, whereas the English rider dismounted and mounted motionless horses. Nevertheless, both riders were cheered to the echo and greeted as heroes. The following day the company left for Hull in Yorkshire, large crowds cheering the train as it sped across England. There was a final performance at Hull on May 5. Then the weary and homesick travelers, amid cheers, boarded the *Persian Monarch,* which set sail at three o'clock in the morning.[51]

The only incident of note on the voyage home was the death of Cody's beloved horse, Old Charlie, who had more than once saved his master's life and who now lay on deck, draped with the American flag until the time came to bury him at sea. Cody was much affected by the horse's death. "We could almost understand each other, and I felt very deeply." The travelers landed at New York at daybreak on May 20 and were greeted by vast applause on Staten Island. Almost at once they were performing again at Erastina. The "Hero of Two Continents," as the New York *Evening Telegram* called him, had come home.[52]

NOTES

1 W. F. Cody, *Story of the Wild West and Camp-Fire Chats* (Philadelphia, 1888; hereafter cited as Cody, *Story*), 706; *Times* (London), April 15, 1887.

2 Capt. F. C. Oppen in an interview with Joseph G. Rosa, May 1977; taped interview with Miss Norah Goodbody in her ninetieth year by Joseph G. Rosa, May 1976.

3 Cody, *Story,* 706–708; *Times* (London), April 15, 1887.

4 Cody, *Story,* 708–711.

5 Nellie Snyder Yost, *Buffalo Bill: His Family, Friends, Failures, and Fortunes* (Chicago, 1979; hereafter cited as Yost, *Buffalo Bill*), 187; "Lord" George Sanger, *Seventy Years a Showman* (London, 1927; hereafter cited as Sanger, *Seventy Years*), passim.

6 Cody, *Story,* 711–713.

7 Ibid.

8 *Daily Telegraph,* April 21, 1887.

9 *Times* (London), April 27, 1887; Laurence Irving, *Henry Irving* (London, 1951), 470.

10 Howard Taubman, *The Making of the American Theater* (New York, 1965), passim.

11 Don Russell, *The Lives and Legends of Buffalo Bill* (Norman, Okla., 1960; hereafter cited as Russell, *Lives*), 334.

12 Cody, *Story,* 724.

13 Ibid., 725–730; *Times* (London), May 6, 1887; *Daily Telegraph,* May 6, 1887.

14 Ibid.

15 Cody, *Story,* 726–728.

16 Ibid., 728; *Times* (London), May 6, 1887; Courtney Ryley Cooper, *Annie Oakley, Woman at Arms* (New York, 1927), 173.

17 Cody, *Story,* 728–730; *Times* (London), May 6, 1887; *Daily Telegraph,* May 6, 1887.

18 Yost, *Buffalo Bill,* 190; Cody, *Story,* 730.

19 W. J. Reader, *Life in Victorian England* (London, 1964), 92; *Times* (London), May 10, 1887.

20 *Leavenworth Times,* January 29, 1889.

21 Cody, *Story,* 733–744.

22 Ibid.

23 *Illustrated London News,* May 14, 1887.

24 Elizabeth Longford, *Queen Victoria* (London, 1964), passim; Cody, *Story,* 734.

25 Cody, *Story,* 734–735.

26 Ibid., 734–737; *Daily Telegraph,* May 12, 1887.

27 Cody, *Story,* 737; *Illustrated London News,* May 21, 1887. The Americans' emotional reaction to the queen's homage to their flag is best understood by the British if they recall that their union flag (commonly called the Union Jack—although "Jack" applies only when the flag is flown on a ship's "Jack-staff") is a national emblem, whereas to most Americans, the "Star Spangled Banner" symbolizes their deep-rooted patriotism and is therefore sacred.

28 Cody, *Story,* 737–738; *Illustrated London News,* May 21, 1887.

29 Queen Victoria's Journal, May 11, 1887, The Royal Archives, Windsor Castle, quoted by gracious permission of Her Majesty Queen Elizabeth II.

30 *Leavenworth Times*, January 29, 1889.

31 Yost, *Buffalo Bill*, 195; *Leavenworth Times*, January 29, 1889.

32 Randolph Churchill, *Winston S. Churchill*, I (London, 1966), 90–92.

33 Cody, *Story*, 739.

34 F. G. Irwin, The North Hotels, to Joseph G. Rosa, February 22, 1978; Yost, *Buffalo Bill*, 198, 466.

35 Ibid., 197–198.

36 Cody, *Story*, 740–744; Russell, *Lives*, 331.

37 Sanger, *Seventy Years*, 187–190.

38 M. Willson Disher, *Greatest Show on Earth* (London, 1937), 264–266.

39 Sanger, *Seventy Years*, 189.

40 *Times* (London), August 25, September 1 and 8, 1887.

41 Sanger, *Seventy Years*, 209; Disher, *Greatest Show on Earth*, 266.

42 Sanger, *Seventy Years*, 209.

43 Yost, *Buffalo Bill*, 200–201.

44 *Times* (London), November 1, 1887.

45 Russell, *Lives*, 337; Annie Fern Swartwout, *Missie* (Blanchester, Ohio, 1947), 142–143, 150–151.

46 Cody, *Story*, 743; Russell, *Lives*, 337–338.

47 Cody, *Story*, 749.

48 Ibid., 750, 756.

49 *Inaugural Invitation Programme*, December 17, 1887.

50 Cody, *Story*, 759–760.

51 Ibid., 763–764; Russell, *Lives*, 340–341.

52 Cody, *Story*, 764–765.

4

INTERNATIONAL TRIUMPHS
AND AN
INDIAN TRAGEDY

The Wild West played at Erastina until mid-August 1888, by which time Cody and no doubt most of his company needed a rest. In Philadelphia, he wrote his sister, he would give only one show a day, then take a month off. So in Richmond, late in October, the Wild West closed, having been on the road for two years and seven months, sea voyages included. Cody did not go straight home to North Platte. He, Burke, and Salsbury and some seventy-five Indians visited Washington, where President Cleveland was suitably impressed. The Indians smoked a pipe of peace at the Bureau of Indian Affairs, then everyone went home at last, the Indians returning to their reservations.[1]

Nebraska in general and North Platte in particular welcomed Cody back warmly, and the local hero could enjoy the sight of his fine new barn with SCOUT'S REST RANCH painted on the roof, as it still is today. An especially pleasing occasion must have been the reception in his honor arranged by the Cody G.A.R. (Grand Army of the Republic) Post of Wallace, which had been organized while the local lion was in England. The veterans had named the post for their Man of the Year, W. F. Cody—an honor indeed, as such posts were usually named for one of the heroic dead. A large party, including Mrs. Cody, Arta, and two English aristocrats, attended the function. A full account of what was surely a mainly happy and relaxed winter has been related by Nebraska's Nellie Yost.[2]

The winter was especially relaxed because there would be no American tour before the Wild West's Parisian engagement. Buffalo Bill saw 1889 in at North Platte and celebrated so well that he was fined one dollar for being drunk and incapable. But he had more important things to occupy him. For some weeks he had been hunting up new acts and attractions in preparation for the French tour. Late in January he was visiting old friends at Leavenworth, where it was reported that he again intended to charter the steamship *Persian Monarch* from New York to France. He planned to take two hundred and fifty people with him—cowboys, Indians, and other performers—together with three hundred head of stock, which would include fifty-seven buffalo from his ranch at North Platte. The Indians were to be Sioux, Cheyenne, and Arapahoe, because they were "more hardy than the others." Cody said that the Indians were only too anxious to go; but bonds for their safe return had to be lodged with the United States government before they could leave their reservations. Cody preferred to take with him Indians who had had little contact with whites, considering that those with such experience would quickly have learned the bad qualities of the white man "without any knowledge of the good, and those, combined with the natural deviltry of the Red man, make him 'heap dam bad.'"[3]

Facsimile of Col. W. F. CODY'S Commission as Brigadier-General in the NATIONAL GUARD (OF THE STATE OF NEBRASKA).

WHEN Cody left for Europe in 1889, he carried with him his commission as an aide-de-camp to the governor of Nebraska, John M. Thayer, with the rank of colonel.

This was later reproduced in the 1893 show program. The original is now at Scout's Rest Ranch. (From the collection of Joseph G. Rosa)

One thing that brightened the horizon was the news that Annie Oakley was back, having had mixed fortunes after her return from Europe, first with a most unwestern outfit run by one Charles Southwell of Philadelphia, whose "cowboys" were anything but. So upon learning that Pawnee Bill could do with a little help at the box office, she and her husband joined him. But after a fair start they suffered from lack of both good contracts and good weather, and Pawnee Bill was

BUFFALO *Bill photographed in Paris in 1889 by Eugene Pirou, who won a medal for his photographic work in the Exposition* *Universelle held that year. (Courtesy Harry Hood)*

unable even to pay his hotel bill at Easton, Maryland. Annie and her Frank were pleased to rejoin Cody for the European tour, though not before she had trod the boards as Sunbeam in a melodrama called *Deadwood Dick.* Pawnee Bill would cross Cody's path again.[4]

On May 19, 1889, the Wild West opened in Paris at the Exposition Universelle, with President Carnot of France there to honor the representatives of France's oldest ally. The engagement was for seven months and was most opportune, for the exposition, together with the celebrations marking the one-hundredth anniversary of the Fall of the Bastille on July 14, 1789, attracted many visitors. Many of them came from Britain, a fact that was not lost on the travel agents. Thomas Cook, already well known for his tours to Europe and the Middle East, arranged it so that his tourists could also take in Buffalo Bill's Wild West or, for those with more bizarre tastes, the occasional public execution when Madame la Guillotine performed her grisly function.

Not surprisingly, the Wild West also attracted a number of artists, all eager to record its unique flavor—unique because no other western entertainment could match it. Among the most famous of these were Frederic Remington and Charles Russell, who, like so many other illustrators, were inspired by the Wild West and Cody in particular. Naturally, a stream of eye-catching posters advertised the show in a realistic manner, and they were to remain popular art of the highest order. Modern posters may be more genuinely artistic perhaps; but in the days before movies and television, posters had to say it all to grab the public, as well as being reasonably accurate. Cody's posters were notably truthful.

Buffalo Bill's looks and figure made him a capital subject for an artist, as the French painter Rosa Bonheur (born in 1822) saw when he came to Paris. Bonheur had spent most of her working life specializing in animal subjects. She enjoyed wide popularity in Britain as well as in France. Her famous 1889 portrait in oil of Cody on horseback now hangs in the Buffalo Bill Historical Center at Cody, Wyoming. There is a glimpse of the artist in old age (made from a photograph) in a poster for the show that dates from 1898. It shows Napoleon Bonaparte and Cody both mounted on horseback, and in the center, the artist, hooded and cloaked, painting the hero of the occasion. It has been claimed, however, that Cody did not approve of the way Bonheur depicted his features, and he secretly commissioned the artist Robert Lindneux to repaint the face! At forty-six, Cody was probably beginning to feel his age, to judge from a letter he wrote to Julia at the time. The social round was clearly becoming a strain, but he feared breaking down before he was out of debt. He wanted to take it easy, and Julia would no doubt sympathize. Doubtless he enjoyed the limelight—why should he not have?—but a rich social life involved many official duties. The day he wrote the letter he had to attend five official functions as well as appear in two shows.[5]

The finest artistic tribute to Buffalo Bill, in the opinion of the authors, is also at Cody. Called simply *The Scout*, it is a masterly, dramatic sculpture, seen at its considerable best at sunset. It is the work of Gertrude Vanderbilt Whitney and dates from 1923. Like the story of the West itself, which is all too often described as romantic, it is truly epic.

Along with Annie Oakley, there had been another return to the show, one that was startling. An Indian who had missed the boat when the rest of the company sailed from Hull for home suddenly appeared in front of Cody in Paris. It was Black Elk, who, with five other Indians, had set out for London after being stranded. They had joined one Mexico Joe's show and had crossed the Channel with him. However, Black Elk fell ill and was looked after by a French lady. When he was better he was told the good news that the Wild West was in town and a fine reunion took place, with Cody leading the assembled company in three rousing cheers. He was asked if he wanted to rejoin the show or go home. He chose the latter, so Cody gave him his ticket home, along with some money and a hearty meal. "Cody had a strong heart," said Black Elk later, and despite what some have claimed, Black Elk's words, reflecting Cody's attitude to his Indians, have never been proved wrong. However, White Horse, one of the Indians who left

the company, invented tales that the Indians were being ill-treated and starved. The *New York Herald* printed the canard, which was soon refuted. American officials in Berlin declared what was evident to all—that they had never seen better-looking or better-fed Indians. However, Cody deemed it better to send the Indians back home in the fall of 1890 in order to satisfy the commissioner of Indian affairs, before which they would have many more European adventures.[6]

After Paris the company visited southern France, then Spain, where the enterprising Major Burke had the Indians photographed beside the statue of Columbus in Barcelona. Disaster now struck the show and the city, in the form of typhoid and Spanish influenza. Several Indians died and so did the show's announcer, Frank Richmond. Annie Oakley was among those taken ill. Naturally, with the city under quarantine, there was a very heavy financial loss. Seven Indians were sent home to recover.[7]

After visiting Corsica and Sardinia, the Wild West reached Naples, to open on January 26, 1890. It arrived in Rome just as Pope Leo XIII was celebrating the twelfth anniversary of his coronation. The entire company lined a corridor along which the pontiff would pass, the Indians magnificent in their finery and Cody carrying off his startling attire— long hair falling over the shoulders of his morning coat—as surely only he could have done. His Holiness blessed the towering American, who bowed deeply. The Indians also bowed to the representative of the Great Spirit on earth, and the Sioux Rocky Bear knelt and made the sign of the cross. The pope seemed touched and blessed the Indians, who became excited and found it hard to remember not to utter a sound.[8]

The company was camped in the Colosseum but could not perform there, as it no longer had a usable arena. The show had an extracurricular triumph on March 4, as the *New York Herald* reported:

All Rome was to-day astir over an attempt of "BUFFALO BILL'S" cowboys with wild horses, which were provided for the occasion by the Prince of Sermoneta.

Several days past the Roman authorities have been busy with the erection of specially-cut barriers for the purpose of keeping back the wild horses from the crowds.

The animals are from the celebrated stud of the Prince of Sermoneta, and the Prince himself declared that no cow-boy in the world could ride these horses. The cow-boys laughed over this surmise, and then offered at least to undertake to mount one of them, if they might choose it.

Every man, woman, and child expected that two or three people would be killed by this attempt.

The anxiety and enthusiasm was great. Over 2,000 carriages were ranged round the field, and more than 20,000 people lined the spacious barriers. Lord Dufferin and many other Diplomatists were on the Terrace.

The epic encounter was something of an anticlimax. The "brutes made springs into the air," it was reported, "but all in vain." It took the cowboys just five minutes to catch and tame the horses, after which they rode them around the arena to enormous applause from the delighted and amused spectators.[9]

The other engagements in Italy were in Florence, Bologna, Milan, Venice, and Verona. The famous photograph of Cody with some of the Indians in a gondola shows them all trying to hold still for the cameraman, as was necessary in those times, especially in a boat. It is not proof, as has been claimed, that the Indians were posing grudgingly. By that token all Victorians were an unhappy lot.[10]

Industrial Milan provided huge audiences over eleven days. One excited watcher was the as yet little-known composer, Giacomo Puccini, who reveled in the show. It is common knowledge among opera buffs that David Belasco's play *The Girl of the Golden West* inspired Puccini's *La Fanciulla del West,* which closely followed it, but Puccini must surely have recalled what he saw that day in 1890. A letter written on April 24 to his brother shows what a deep impression the show made on him.[11]

At Verona the Wild West had its grandest setting of all, the mighty Roman amphitheater, which today houses the

BUFFALO *Bill took second place to the king of Bavaria and his daughters when they* *visited the Wild West in Munich on April 24, 1890. (Courtesy Scout's Rest Ranch)*

largest of all open-air opera festivals. Cody was able to use the actual arena— where part of the opera audience sits— for his show, which was as grand and exciting as the original carnivals held there were bloody. Perhaps forty-five thousand watched the Wild West that day.[12]

Now the Wild West moved on to Germany, where it spent much of 1890–91. The enthusiasm engendered by the show seems to have been greater in Germany than anywhere else in Europe, and it had one significant result. A member of the public was clearly so smitten by the prowess and splendor on display that he started on a career which, to quote the *Encyclopedia Americana,* has made him

"one of the world's all-time fiction best sellers."

The name of this prodigy is little known in English-speaking countries; but on the Continent Karl May still has a vast following. Born in 1842 to a weaver, May became a schoolmaster but was imprisoned for theft. In fact, he spent much of the next thirteen years in and out of prison for various frauds and swindles. Upon his release in 1874, he regarded himself as a social outcast. That same year, however, he started to write, and between 1887 and 1900, armed with atlases and encyclopedias and other reference works, he began his career as a writer of western and oriental novels.

Cody inspired many of the stories, but May's greatest successes featured such characters as "Old Shatterhand" and other God-fearing individuals. By the early years of this century May began to imply that many of the adventures he wrote about were based on his own life. This led to a close examination of his past, and when his criminal record was revealed, his reputation suffered. May died in 1912, but his stories continued to fascinate generations of Germans. His many admirers included Albert Schweitzer, Albert Einstein, and one Adolf Hitler.

Today, Karl May's books still sell well, and there is a museum in Munich devoted to his life and work. The museum also boasts some Buffalo Bill treasures, notably a painting of Custer's Last Stand by the German artist Elk Eber, who obtained first-hand details from a Sioux woman who had witnessed part of the battle. She later accompanied Buffalo Bill to Germany, where she met and married a German.

The appetite for the Old West remains strong among Germans, and this continuing interest shows the extent of Cody's influence. The authors know of only one serious organization in Britain devoted to the study of the real West, and that is the English Westerners' Society. Germany boasts at least seven. On a more popular level, there are parks where Germans can imagine themselves back in the Old West. Though little known in America or Britain, Karl May was one of the most successful writers of fiction in history. Like Cody, he was a trailblazer. Unlike Cody, he died phenomenally rich.[13]

A winter season was planned for southern France and the Riviera, but, as noted earlier, something had to be done to combat the continuing rumors of mistreatment of the show's Indians. Before considering how Cody successfully quashed the false charges against him, it must be stated that the well-meaning officials of the Bureau of Indian Affairs, because they believed in the assimilation of the Indian into American life, objected to Cody and his Wild West—the crucial Indian part of it—on principle. John Oberley, commissioner of Indian affairs in the final period of President Cleveland's first administration, wrote thus in 1889:

> The effect of traveling all over the country among, and associated with, the class of people usually accompanying Shows, Circuses and Exhibitions, attended by all the immoral and unchristianizing surroundings incident to such a life, is not only most demoralizing to the present and future welfare of the Indian, but it creates a roaming and unsettled disposition and educates him in a manner entirely foreign and antagonistic to that which has been and now is the policy of the Government.[14]

One cannot deride such honestly held opinions; few employers can have been as scrupulous as were Cody and Salsbury.

BUFFALO Bill ca. 1890. This pose has inspired a number of artists. It also became
one of the original transplants—Cody's head
was removed and replaced by Wild Bill

Hickok's in a particularly bizarre effort by
White ca. 1892. (Courtesy Buffalo Bill Historical Center)

One can appreciate Oberley's sentiments. If Cody had not been such a true friend to his Indians—which in itself made him something of a phenomenon—it would be possible to side with the bureau's attitude. Deaths in a far-off country could seem from a distance to be due to lack of care. While the flames of controversy were fanned by certain eastern newspapers despite lack of evidence from Europe, the journalists climbed onto a natural bandwagon. Against this background, and because the Indians often fell victim to the diseases to which they were exposed in foreign lands regardless of their treatment by whites, Cody's decision to send his Indians home became inevitable. [15]

The rest of the Wild West's personnel settled in winter quarters at Benfeld in Alsace-Lorraine. Meanwhile, Burke and the Indians arrived in Philadelphia on November 13, 1890. Herbert Walsh, the secretary of the Indian Rights Association, was ordered by Acting Commissioner Belt—Commissioner Morgan was away—to examine the Indians, but Burke acted quickly and took them to Washington. There they met senators, congressmen, the secretary of the interior, and other officials. The result, not surprisingly, was a vindication of Cody and his staff. No Indians complained. All praised Cody and his show, and the deaths were explained by the Indians themselves. Their dead comrades had been unhealthy when they set out; the agency doctor had failed in his duty.

Wounds One Another, who died after falling from a moving train in Germany, had, the Indians said, been drunk at the time. That was the end of the matter. Salsbury wrote off Walsh and company as benevolent cranks. [16]

Events of a more serious nature now intervened. Cody had planned to join Burke in Washington, but when he reached New York there was a telegram waiting for him from General Miles urging Cody to meet him in Chicago at once. Cody was there within thirty-six hours. [17]

The background of the crisis that led to Wounded Knee (the wretchedness on the Sioux reservations, with the despairing Indians who believed that the Ghost Dance would restore the old days to them and free them from the whites) is not the immediate concern of this book. General Miles, who appeared to think that the threat was greater than that of Pontiac or Tecumseh in earlier times, believed that Cody could bring Sitting Bull—alleged to be behind the troubles—to Standing Rock to parley with him. He asked Cody to go to Sitting Bull's camp, which lay some fifty miles from the Standing Rock Agency, and wait for Miles himself to appear. [18]

Cody believed that he could bring his old friend in. Unfortunately, James Mc-Laughlin, though a friend of the Indians, knew little about them and, more seriously, little about the great Sitting Bull. The agent would character assassinate him later in print. McLaughlin liked "tame" Indians, so he appealed to the commissioner of Indian affairs, telegraphing him that Cody had arrived with a commission from Miles to arrest Sitting Bull. He claimed that the step was unnecessary, as it would precipitate a fight. A few Indians were still dancing, but the agent did not consider that bloodshed would result. At the appropriate moment, he wanted to be the man to arrest Sitting Bull. He ended: "Request Gen. Miles' order to Cody be rescinded and request immediate answer."[19]

McLaughlin had allies in the officers at Fort Yates. These officers were Eighth Cavalry and Twelfth Infantry men, who knew of Cody only by repute. Don Russell suggests that they may have regarded him as a mere showman and dime-novel hero, which seems likely. As a showman he was never out of the papers. The officers certainly misjudged his drinking capacity, for they imagined that they could render him drunk and incapable. Assistant Surgeon Alonzo R. Chapin's comment on the proceedings is Homeric: "Colonel Cody's capacity was such that it took practically all the officers in details of two or three at a time to keep him interested and busy through the day."[20]

After a good night's sleep Cody left the post with Pony Bob Haslam, White Beaver Powell, Bully White, and Steve Burke—but without reporters. There was no hurry. Indeed, they heard at one point that Sitting Bull was actually on his way to the agency. Meanwhile, a Chicago

THE *legendary Sitting Bull ca. 1885 during the time he made a brief appearance with Buffalo Bill's Wild West. The pair struck up a friendship based on mutual respect. (Courtesy Smithsonian Institution, National Anthropological Archives)*

journalist was photographing a ghost dance, an action hardly possible if McLaughlin's lurid stories were true. Unfortunately, Cody's moment had come, for President Harrison, having received McLaughlin's version of the affair, demanded Cody's return. So it happened that Cody never saw Sitting Bull. The tragic outcome need only be summarized here. Miles ordered the arrest of Sitting Bull and of Chief Big Foot, who would die at Wounded Knee. Indian police and troops were sent to Sitting Bull's tent at dawn on December 15, 1890. The great Sioux was seized. His people tried to rescue him, but in the fight that ensued he was shot dead by Sergeant Red Tomahawk.[21]

There was a moment of dramatic irony during the firing, for the horse that Cody had given Sitting Bull started to perform his tricks. Those watching thought that the horse was performing the Ghost Dance, but then he stopped and walked away from the tragic scene. The fighting began again and continued until cavalry rode to the rescue of the Indian police. The horse was ridden to Fort Yates, bringing the news of Sitting Bull's death. (It was returned to Cody and was ridden

BUFFALO *Bill and Sitting Bull photographed by W. Notman, Montreal, in 1885. D. F. Barrie copied this photograph and placed his own copyright on prints or perhaps purchased Notman's original glass plates. (Courtesy Buffalo Bill Historical Center)*

by the standard-bearer when the Wild West was at the Chicago Columbian Exposition in 1893.)[22]

On December 29, 1890, the Indian Wars ended in the partly tragic accident, partly bloody shambles that was Wounded Knee.[23]

Cody did not have long to relax at North Platte after his abortive attempt to reach Sitting Bull. In November 1889, he had been commissioned an aide-de-camp on the staff of Governor John M. Thayer of Nebraska, with the rank of brigadier general. On January 6, 1891, Thayer put him to work:

As you are a member of my Staff, I have detailed you for special services; the particular nature of which was made known during our conversation.

You will proceed to the scene of the Indian troubles and communicate with General Miles.

You will in addition to the special service refer[r]ed to, please visit the different towns, if time permit [sic], along the line of the Elkhorn Rail-Road, and use your influence to quiet excitement and remove apprehensions upon the part of the people.

Please call upon General Colby, and give him your views as to the probability of the Indians breaking through the cordon of regular troops; your superior knowledge of Indian character and mode of warfare, may enable you to make suggestions of importance.

All Officers and members of the State Troops, and all others, will please extend to you every courtesy.[24]

The exact nature of the "special service" that was required of Cody is unknown. Don Russell has suggested that it was to help quench any irresponsible actions by a local militia officer along the Nebraska border—General Miles was eager to avoid a general outbreak. Fortunately, no such trouble occurred, and Cody came to the Pine Ridge Agency. Major Burke was there with the Wild West's Indians, who were serving as Indian police. Dr. Royer, the Pine Ridge agent, was ordered to examine them. This was the final vindication of Cody's treatment of his charges, for there was nothing but praise for him and for Burke for their treatment of the Indians abroad. The *New York Herald* carried an article by Cody on Indians' rights and the good prospects of peace, which came on January 16 with the formal surrender of the unfortunate "hostiles." Cody took part in a grand review of the troops. Though he had many more years ahead of him as a roving unofficial ambassador for his country, the review was his last act in the service of his government.[25]

It will be recalled that Nate Salsbury

was still in Europe. Realizing that he might not have Indians available, he was busily planning a new version of the show, which would soon be called "Buffalo Bill's Wild West and Congress of Rough Riders of the World." This grandiloquent title indicated a change of emphasis, but not a drastic one, apart from the use of foreign troops. Rough Riders was a fairly common western expression. An Illinois cavalry regiment had been called "rough riders," while the bronco buster with the toughest assignment was said to be "riding the rough string."[26]

The new program contained mostly old favorites, but new features included a grand review of American, British, French, German, and Russian troops, Syrian and Arab horsemen, and military evolutions by a company of each of the following: 20 men of the U.S. Sixth Cavalry; 20 of the Twelfth Lancers (Prince of Wales' Regiment); 20 of the First Guard Uhlan Regiment of the German Emperor; 20 French Chasseurs; 12 Cossacks; 6 Argentinian gauchos; and the old hands—cowboys, cowgirls, vaqueros, the cowboy mounted band and—this time—100 Sioux. The western element was not demoted, but there was an extra emphasis on horsemanship.[27]

This new Wild West opened in 1891 in Germany, where it helped improve the efficiency of the German army. The extreme professionalism of the Wild West's management was studied by German officers, notebooks in hand, not least the swift "set-up" after rapid unloading from the show's train. Annie Oakley noted this intense interest, which would pay dividends in 1914. The company got three hot meals a day, and the expertise needed to provide them perhaps resulted in well-fed German troops in World War I. Annie Oakley would later regret the fact that she had so accurately shot the ash from the cigarette of the kaiser-to-be when she appeared in Berlin after the first visit to London.[28]

Show members visited Holland and Belgium. They included a trip to the battlefield of Waterloo, where they raised the American flag. Queen Wilhelmina of the Netherlands, who had seen the Wild West in 1887 in London, made the Americans welcome. Then it was back to Britain once more. The most emotional moment in a triumphant reconquest of Britain was a special performance in Manchester to aid the survivors of the Light Brigade, some of whom had fallen on hard times. Nineteen of the "brave six hundred" who had ridden into immortality when they charged the Russian guns at Balaclava on October 25, 1854, during the Crimean War, were present. The event was an enormous success. It is reasonable to assume that the old show-business cliché was genuinely true that day and that there was "not a dry eye in the house." They visited Stoke-on-Trent, capital of the "Potteries," and like everyone else before or since, the Indians were able to marvel at Wedgwood china in the making and on display. Cardiff, capital of Wales, provided the best box office returns the Wild West had ever enjoyed for a six-day stand, while another highlight—an emotional one—was the occasion in Glasgow when, at the sight of the Stars and Stripes, six thousand orphans sang "Yankee Doodle."[29]

Cody left the show that winter to return to North Platte. He had not felt fit for some time, and the strain of constant touring and being in the public eye on and offstage was clearly beginning to tell. The company split into two; Thern Camfield organized part of the group to perform in theaters, while the rest of the company performed Mackaye's indoor pageant once more, this time in Glasgow's East End Exhibition Building. Elephants were hired from France and, even more exotically, thirty Zulu warriors and thirty Zulu women were hired from Henry M. ("Doctor Livingstone, I presume?") Stanley, who had brought them to Hamburg. Upon arriving in Glasgow the Zulus were assembled. At the urging of the press photographers, they faced the Indians. Bronco Bill asked Rocky Bear to try out the Indians' sign language on the Zulus. He did so, and the Zulu chief answered him.[30]

Meanwhile, Cody reached home. Al Goodman was hard at work completing the big new barn and buying bulls from the best bloodlines—the barn was big enough to shelter all the stock through the winter. Arta Cody had married Horton Boal, and the newlyweds wished to run the ranch. With Mrs. Cody on their side, they got their wish, and Al Good-

man and Julia left for Kansas. It could have been a more peaceful vacation for Cody, but at least he was offstage for a time, out of the public view. Not that the show was forgotten; individuals, horses, and new acts were hired. Then, early in 1892, Cody returned to Europe.[31]

The new season commenced at Earl's Court in London on May 7, 1892, complete with new horses that Cody had brought back. No doubt a repeat of the 1887 Wild West would have gone down well, but there were enough new acts to ensure great enthusiasm, particular favorites being Prince Ivan Rostomov Macheradse and his cossacks. Two of the many who commentated on the new show were Queen Victoria and the artist Frederic Remington, who could look at the spectacle with a professional eye. Remington noted that all visitors to London went first to the Wild West, and he alleged that all cab drivers headed there as soon as they picked up their fare. Where else would a fellow go? Remington went on to show that he was a good journalist as well as a fine artist:

> The Tower, the Parliament, and Westminster are older institutions than Buffalo Bill's show, but when the New Zealander sits on the London Bridge and looks over his ancient manuscripts of Murray's Guide-book he is going to turn first to the Wild West. At present everyone knows where it is, from the gentleman on Piccadilly to the dirtiest coster in the remotest slum of White-

chapel. The Cabman may have to scratch his head to recall places where the traveller desires to go, but when the Wild West is asked for he gathers his reins and uncoils his whip without ceremony.[32]

The queen's visit to the show—a command performance at Windsor Castle on June 26—was officially recorded in the court circular column of the *Times* the following day. However, her own account in her journal, written that evening, is of more interest:

We went on to the East Terrace, & watched from a tent, open in front, a sort of "Buffalo Bill" performance, on the lawn below. It was extremely well arranged, & an excellent representation of what we had also seen 5 years ago at Earl's Court. There were Cow Boys, Red Indians, Mexicans, Argentinos taking part, & then a wonderful riding display by Cossacks, accompanied by curious singing, & a war dance by the Indians. There was extraordinary buck jumping horses, shooting at glass balls by Col: Cody (Buffalo Bill), & display of cracking huge long whips. The whole, was a very pretty wild sight, which lasted an hour. At the conclusion of the performance, all advanced in line at a gallop & stopped suddenly. Col: Cody was brought up for me to speak to him. He is still a very handsome man, but has now got a grey beard.[33]

The queen had particularly wished to see the cossacks, whose act lasted a bare twelve minutes. Nate Salsbury had decided that as they could hardly constitute a show and would be hardly worth the trouble of getting them there, an hour's performance would be in order. Burke was clearly in good form that day. Salsbury noted that he had let his hair down and, therefore, "we knew the afternoon was bound to be a success, for whenever the Major let his hair down the world stood in awe."[34]

Salsbury acted as commentator to Her Majesty at her request, or, as he later put it, "I nobly threw myself into the breech, and was escorted with much ceremony" to a pavilion, where he acted as "Scout, Guide and Interpreter." There was a strong draft, and the queen urged him to put his hat on. When she asked what weapon the colonel was using, he told her that it was "the Winchester rifle, Madame, an American firearm."

"Ah!" exclaimed the queen, "a very effective weapon and in very effective hands."[35]

When the cossacks were performing, the queen's son-in-law, Prince Henry of Battenberg, asked the queen in German if she thought that they really were cossacks. Before she could reply, Salsbury broke in to assure her that everything and everyone was genuine. Amused, the queen remarked to her son-in-law: "Prince, I think we had better speak English for the rest of the afternoon." Princess Beatrice, and the queen, amused at the prince's discomfort, noted in French that he had received his first American lesson. Salsbury now triumphed again, breaking in with "Oh, Madam, j'espère non!" There was a general laugh, and the happy Salsbury was only sorry that Burke was not beside him to see and hear his triumph.[36]

After the performance Cody and Salsbury were taken to the equerry's apartments and invited to have lunch. Salsbury later wrote: "We compromised by another act of self-sacrifice on my part, for as Cody did not drink anything that summer, I did my duty for both of us in a glass of wine." Cody was given "a beautiful watch charm" and Salsbury a scarf pin set in diamonds, with the royal monogram on it. He committed this piece of social comment to paper: "Our experience that afternoon proved to me that the higher you ascend the social scale in England, the more delightful do you find the surroundings. During the entire afternoon there was an utter absence of what a Montana lady would call 'lugs.'"[37]

The London season closed on October 12, 1892. Nothing could match the impact of the 1887 season, but this second visit was undoubtedly another outright triumph. So ended a European tour that had spanned almost three-and-a-half years. The next target was the World's Columbian Exposition in Chicago, which was to open in the spring of 1893. Nate Salsbury learned that the show was not to be housed on the actual exposition site, so he leased a site near its entrance,

through which some visitors went by mistake—and came out satisfied. This is not to denigrate the exposition, which Chicagoan Don Russell believed "probably rates the highest in general interest and lasting influence" of all the world fairs. Yet Russell quotes a Chicago city editor who considered the 1893 Wild West to be the greatest show he had ever seen.[38]

The Wild West had fifteen acres to use, and a grandstand was built to house eighteen thousand. Since 1887 Europe had seen far more of the show than had the United States, where a single season had been given. Cody's overseas triumphs; the failure of his self-righteous opponents to prove that he was harming the well-being of his Indians; his—in modern parlance—high profile final Indian campaign, even if he had failed in his objective; his potent star quality—all added to the impact of a magnificent spectacle of entertainment. Like hundreds of thousands of Europeans, Americans enjoyed wandering about Cody's camp, which was well run and which boasted a glamorous mixture of nationalities. Like the artist Rosa Bonheur in France, Amy Leslie of the *Chicago Daily News* spent much time with Cody and his closest associates, also with Irma and Arta. She has left us a most attractive portrait of him:

No such an engaging story-teller as Buffalo Bill figures in history or romance. He is quiet, rich in humor and mellow as a bottle of old port . . . and

COL. W. F. CODY. —:: AND ::— NATE SALSBURY.

BUFFALO BILL'S
WILD WEST

CONGRESS OF ROUGH RIDERS OF THE WORLD.

Programme

OVERTURE, "Star Spangled Banner" · · COWBOY BAND, WM. SWEENY, Leader

1—GRAND REVIEW introducing the Rough Riders of the World and Fully Equipped Regular Soldiers of the Armies of America, England, France, Germany, and Russia.

2—MISS ANNIE OAKLEY, Celebrated Shot, who will illustrate her dexterity in the use of Fire-arms.

3—HORSE RACE between a Cowboy, a Cossack, a Mexican, an Arab, and an Indian, on Spanish-Mexican, Broncho, Russian, Indian and Arabian Horses.

4—PONY EXPRESS. The Former Pony Post Rider will show how the Letters and Telegrams of the Republic were distributed across the immense Continent previous to the Railways and the Telegraph.

5—ILLUSTRATING A PRAIRIE EMIGRANT TRAIN CROSSING THE PLAINS. Attack by marauding Indians repulsed by "Buffalo Bill," with Scouts and Cowboys.
   N. B.—The Wagons are the same as used 35 years ago.

6—A GROUP OF SYRIAN AND ARABIAN HORSEMEN will illustrate their style of Horsemanship, with Native Sports and Pastimes.

7—COSSACKS, of the Caucasus of Russia, in Feats of Horsemanship, Native Dances, etc.

8—JOHNNY BAKER, Celebrated Young American Marksman.

9—A GROUP OF MEXICANS from Old Mexico, will illustrate the use of the Lasso, and perform various Feats of Horsemanship,

10—RACING BETWEEN PRAIRIE, SPANISH AND INDIAN GIRLS.

11—COWBOY FUN. Picking Objects from the Ground, Lassoing Wild Horses, Riding the Buckers.

12—MILITARY EVOLUTIONS by a Company of the Sixth Cavalry of the United States Army; a Company of the First Guard Uhlan Regiment of His Majesty King William II, German Emperor, popularly known as the "Potsdamer Reds"; a Company of French Chasseurs (Chasseurs a Cheval de la Garde Republique Francaise); and a Company of the 12th Lancers (Prince of Wales' Regiment) of the British Army.

13—CAPTURE OF THE DEADWOOD MAIL COACH BY THE INDIANS, which will be rescued by "Buffalo Bill" and his attendant Cowboys.
   N. B.—This is the identical old Deadwood Coach, called the Mail Coach, which is famous on account of having carried the great number of people who lost their lives on the road between Deadwood and Cheyenne 18 years ago. Now the most famed vehicle extant.

14—RACING BETWEEN INDIAN BOYS ON BAREBACK HORSES.

15—LIFE CUSTOMS OF THE INDIANS. Indian Settlement on the Field and "Path."

16—COL. W. F. CODY, ("Buffalo Bill"), in his Unique Feats of Sharpshooting.

17—BUFFALO HUNT, as it is in the Far West of North America—"Buffalo Bill" and Indians. The last of the only known Native Herd.

18—ATTACK ON A SETTLER'S CABIN, capture by the Indians. Rescue by "Buffalo Bill" and the Cowboys.

19—SALUTE. CONCLUSION

THE 1893 "Programme." Item 18, An attack on a Settler's Cabin, has been overstamped with Battle of the Little Big Horn, or Custer's Last Charge, for this performance. (From the collection of Joseph G. Rosa)

not a dozen men I know have his splendid magnetism, keen appreciation and happy originality. He sticks to the truth mainly and is more intensely beguiling than the veriest makers of fiction.[39]

A high spot of the year was the Thousand Mile Cowboy Race, conceived by riders in the Nebraska cowtown of Chadron and in Sturgis, South Dakota, who felt like visiting the great event in Chicago. This idea was extended and changed. Now it would publicize the remarkable stamina and speed of the western horse. Chadron put up $1,000 for prize money. Cody added $500, with the proviso that the race should end at the Wild West's entrance. Another prize was a saddle. The object was to beat a previous record by French horses of fifty miles a day. The organizers set thirteen days for the race at an average of seventy-five miles a day. Every rider had two horses with him, one ridden, the other led. Horse lovers did not like the idea, and the governor of Illinois banned the race. The organizers got around the ban, however, when representatives of humanitarian societies were asked to oversee the proceedings.[40]

There were eight, nine, or ten entrants, and the race itself is as vaguely chronicled as that absurdly vague statement. One John Berry was the victor in thirteen days and sixteen hours. He had his detractors. They claimed that he had sent his horses by express and taken a train for the first hundred miles and anyway knew the route because he had helped lay it out. Having cheated, he was given only a saddle. The prize money was divided up by those who had finished legitimately, one George Jones getting the lion's share for being the fastest. Space forbids more details of the shady goings-on. Yet there was an excellent sequel, for the massive publicity not only boosted Cody but also the stamina of the western horse. The British and French in particular were interested in the breed for light cavalry horses.[41]

The show as seen in Chicago would remain mainly unchanged for nearly a decade. It closed in the city on October 31, 1892, reopening in Brooklyn on May 12, 1894, for a five-month season. Cody's ailing marriage had not been helped by an incident in Chicago when Louisa came to visit him. Cody was not expecting her; the visit was to be a surprise. Louisa appeared at his hotel, only to be told that she would be taken to Mr. and Mrs. Cody's suite. The Mrs. Cody in residence was possibly "the finest looking woman in the world"—which is what Cody called

the British actress, Katherine Clemmons, whom he had met on his first visit to Britain. He would later stage a play for her in America, which flopped. Whoever it was, Louisa was understandably upset, though she must have known only too well that her handsome, famous husband was a natural magnet for some members of the opposite sex. Cody made amends by giving his wife the deeds of the finest house in North Platte.[42]

The 1894 season in New York had a new attraction, South American gauchos. These Primitive Riders bestrode "Western Bronco ponies that had never jumped a hurdle until three days before the opening of the present exhibition," so the audiences were told. The Brooklyn grandstand held twenty thousand, but attendance was not good enough, and Cody's affairs back in Nebraska did not prosper either. He had been virtually a millionaire in 1893 but was in dire straits less than a year later. Another blow was the illness of Nate Salsbury, who was never able to manage the Wild West's affairs again except in an advisory capacity. James A. Bailey of Barnum and Bailey fame—Barnum had died in 1891—made a deal with Cody; he would take a share of the profits in return for providing transport and local expenses.[43]

Philadelphia saw the new team in action for the first time on April 22, 1895. The engagement finished on May 4, after which a rugged period began, a 190-day trek with 131 stands, covering nine thousand miles. The trail ended at Atlanta,

THEY *would not dare do it today. Photographed in the early 1900s, these Sioux Indians are performing their "dog-eating" ceremony at Madison Square Garden. High-* *speed cameras were still to come, as can be seen from the blurred effect of the dancers. (Courtesy Buffalo Bill Historical Center)*

Georgia, on November 2. Using fifty-two cars—more than either Ringling or Barnum and Bailey used—Bailey masterminded the tour. Despite his illness, Salsbury, too, was acting, presenting "Black America," a deep-South version of the Wild West. This was put together by a minstrel show expert, Lew Parker, complete with three hundred black show people who traveled in fifteen railway cars. The shrewd Salsbury decided that the idea would not work, but he was overruled by Cody. Salsbury was right.

The idea was misconceived, and the show flopped. However, Cody's own Wild West succeeded yet again, though his health suffered. His fame increased, however, for the one-night stands brought the show to a huge public. There were 132 stops in 1896, 104 in 1897, but without Salsbury, and with increasing age and much ill-health, Cody was sorely taxed. One-night stands, with so much expected of the star of stars, was a long-term feat of endurance for a fifty-year-old.[44]

A few big cities on this tour had runs

COL. W. F. CODY, Prop. H. S. BOAL, Manager.

SCOUT'S REST STOCK RANCH,

CHAS. TREGO, Ranch Foreman.
J. W. BOYER, Farm Foreman.

—BREEDERS OF—

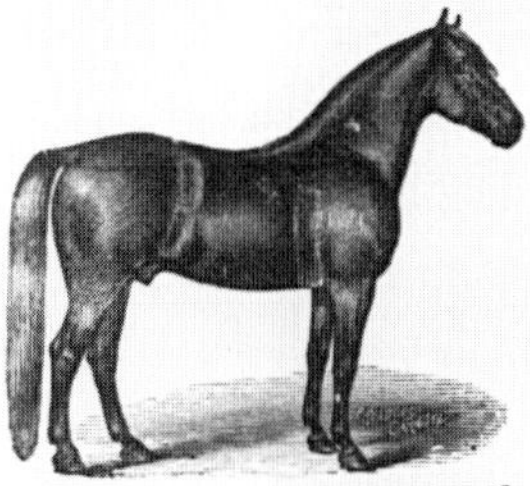

Cleveland Bay and Clydesdale Horses,

—ALSO—

Hereford and Shorthorn Cattle.

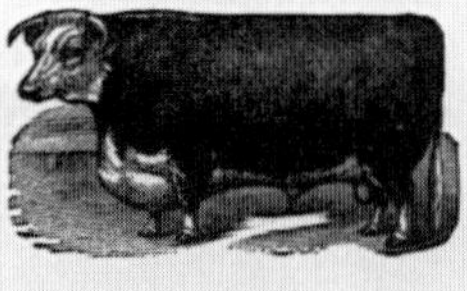

North Platte, Neb., Feb 28th 1894

Capt Charles Penney
Act Agt Pine Ridge
Dear Captain.

I presume you were informed by the Interior Dept. That I have permission for Indians, I am writing Shangrau. And I dont wish to commence looking up Indians. Until I have your permission so if you see Shangrau will you please speak to him about it I will not want the Indians much before May. but its well to be letting them know. I will try my best to come after them myself.

With my best wishes
Yours truly
W. F. Cody

PERIODICALLY, *Cody was required to approach the Bureau of Indian Affairs or the Pine Ridge Agency concerning the recruitment of Indians for the Wild West. This letter, written in 1894, confirms that he needed Indians for his new season and that he hoped to visit the agency himself. (Courtesy Federal Records Center, Kansas City, Missouri)*

of from two to five nights; but more typical was the first week of July 1896: Kokomo, Bluffton, and Marion, Indiana; Piqua, Dayton, and Springfield, Ohio. Much of Cody's money was being sent back to Nebraska and to Wyoming, where he hoped to build a big irrigation canal. He even organized a peace treaty between the Sioux and the Chippewas, who had, in fact, been at peace for many years but who had never officially ceased their struggle. The Sioux representatives were part of the Wild West. The place was Ashland, Wisconsin, and the treaty stuck.[45]

In 1897, the Wild West gave New Yorkers fresh attractions in keeping with the times. Drill was then all the rage, complete with fanciful titles such as The Modern Woodmen of America, but Cody had more professional versions, notably drill by U.S. artillerymen and men of the Sixth Cavalry. Zouave infantry drill, a series of striking sequences in double time, was presented. Veterans of the Spanish-American War, who had been given leave to allow their wounds to heal, also appeared. Cody's disappointment over his failure to get to Cuba will be discussed later.[46]

It is sentimental to lament the change from the old and truly western Wild West of the early days, because though the public wanted and was given novelties, many features remained constant, as will be seen, to the end. Others were getting into the western act now, including one Colonel Cummings (who later appeared in London with the aging Red Shirt as a main attraction). Cummings was presenting nothing as common as a "Wild West show," but a "serious ethnological exhibition." Cummings also visited other parts of Europe besides Britain, and it is reported that during one of his American tours, Calamity Jane (Martha Jane Cannary) made a brief appearance with his show. Contradictions notwithstanding, however—including a fake diary that first appeared in 1941—Jane was never with Cody's Wild West. Even Geronimo and Chief Joseph appeared with Cummings. Space forbids a complete breakdown of all the western-type shows that abounded at the turn of the century. That only *one* is remembered in any detail and with much affection is proof that it was the best. Of course, the flood of Buffalo Bill dime novels—557, according to the indefatigable Don Russell—added to the fame of the genuine article, however absurd their content might be.[47]

Colonel Tim McCoy, born in Saginaw, Michigan, but a genuine Wyoming cowboy who became a Hollywood star be-

tween the wars, has left us a vivid account of his boyhood encounter with
Cody when the Wild West played his
birthplace on July 16, 1898. Although
the show was thrilling, there was a
greater treat in store. Young Tim's father
was the town's chief of police and saw to
it that they met the great man. McCoy
never forgot that day of days:

> He sat in his tent, holding court in a
> dark cutaway coat. His shirt was
> trimmed with the kind of long collar
> worn today, only he was wearing it
> then. Around his neck was a four-hand
> tie half a size larger than is fashionable
> now, and in that tie was a stickpin
> with the three feathers of the Prince of
> Wales, given to him as a token by the
> Prince when he was touring England.

For McCoy, Cody was "the most impressive man I had ever seen, unmatched
either before or since. As someone once
said, he was the 'greatest one man tab-
leau that ever lived.'"[48]
Naturally, Cody hoped to take part in
the Spanish-American War, which had
broken out in April 1898. He at once offered his services, including four hundred
horses and a company of cavalry scouts
that he would raise. His old friend General Miles was keen to have him, but the
general did not reach Cuba until late in
July and the small war was over by mid-
August. Miles had in fact sent for Cody
in late July, but when he heard how
much it would cost to close the show, he

told Cody to stay at home. At this time it
seems absurd that a man in his fifties
should feel obliged to rush into action. A
letter Cody wrote home sums up his position as he, and no doubt others, saw it
then. He wrote to a friend that he would
have a hard time leaving the show "but if
I don't go—I will be damned forever by
all—I must go—or lose my reputation."
He said his heart was not in the war, but
that he must stand by America. Of additional interest is the fact that on April
20, 1898, Cody literally "went on record"
when he made a recording for the Ber-
liner Gramophone Company in which he
stressed the need to send troops if war
broke out (which it did, four days later).
He urged all Americans to support the
president. And at the end, probably finding himself with seconds to spare, he
said, "Ladies and gentlemen, permit me
to introduce to you a Congress of the
Rough Riders of the World." Cody's
strong, resonant voice, echoing as it does
down the years, must surely be music to
the ears of any red-blooded historian or
lover of the Old West![49]
In truth, Cody's first duty was not patriotism, but to the show—and he was
not damned forever. The year was a good
one for him. Omaha held a major exhibition, the Trans-Mississippi Exposition,
and the local hero was honored at it on
August 31. This was Cody Day. The great
man and his company performed at the
very spot where the Wild West had been
inaugurated back in 1883. Nebraskans
hailed him, as Nellie Yost has written,

BUFFALO *Bill inspects his Indian friends prior to a performance.*

(Courtesy Scout's Rest Ranch)

"with a recognition and an ovation that has probably never been equalled." The venerable Alexander Majors was on hand to speak of the little boy who had been brought to him "forty-three years ago to this day" asking for employment of some kind. Few present knew that Majors had survived because Cody gave him a regular allowance. Then it was North Platte's turn to hail the conquering hero once more.[50]

In September Cody caught typhoid fever and fainted three times during a performance. The season was nearly over, however, and it ended at Charleston, West Virginia, on October 15, 1898, allowing Cody to recuperate that winter at North Platte.[51]

The Wild West of 1899 inevitably included sixteen of Teddy Roosevelt's Rough Riders and the Battle of San Juan Hill. Some Cubans, Hawaiians, and Filipinos—eighteen in all—took part, to the huge delight of the public that year

THIS *photograph, ca. 1900, depicts left to right: Johnny Baker, Nate Salsbury, Iron Tail, Cody, and Mrs. Rachel Salsbury. Iron Tail was the "war chief" and head of all the Wild West Indians. It is generally believed that Iron Tail was James Earle Fraser's model for the Indian head on the "buffalo nickel," but Fraser claimed that the final design was based on Iron Tail and Two Moon. Nate's haggard appearance may be the result of his failing health. His subsequent death in*

1902 was a personal loss for Cody, and, as events were to prove, a disaster for the Wild West. (Courtesy Buffalo Bill Historical Center) ABOVE

THE *Concordia (Kans.) Blade carried this advertisement in its issue of September 20, 1900. It shows graphically how Cody kept the Wild West up-to-date. (Courtesy Kansas State Historical Society)* RIGHT

Concordia One Day Only Saturday Sept. 29.

THE HERO HORSEMEN OF TWO HEMISPHERES

"Last Year's Wonders all Surpassed, Last and Best and Best at Last."

A Pre-Babel Congregation of Men Representing All Races, All Nations, All Tongues

The Living, Breathing, Lexicographical Definer of the Words, Courage, Dash, Daring and Skill, is

BUFFALO BILL'S WILD WEST

Congress of Rough Riders of the World

UNDER THE PERSONAL COMMAND OF COL. WM. F. CODY, "BUFFALO BILL."

600 MEN! 500 HORSES!

The program replete with thrilling historical episodes, contests in skill and daring, feats of horsemanship and marksmanship, including a reproduction of that superlatively superior and accurately detailed BATTLE SCENE, representing the

CHARGE UP SAN JUAN HILL

BY ROOSEVELT'S ROUGH RIDERS

And U. S. Regulars and Volunteer Soldiers (white and colored), and Veterans of the Cuban Army, genuine participants in the actual

FIGHTING AT SANTIAGO.

COL. W.F. CODY
(BUFFALO BILL)
PRESIDENT.

AMERICAN COWBOYS—In feats of Horsemanship and Sports of the Plains.

MEXICAN VAQUEROS—In National Pastimes, lariat throwing and riding.

MISS ANNIE OAKLEY—"Little Sure-Shot", in Feats of Skill.

SOUTH AMERICAN GAUCHOS—Illustrating the Horsemanship and Bolas Throwing.

RUSSIAN COSSACKS—The Free Lances of the Russian Steppes.

RIFFIAN ARABS—Sons of the Boundless Desert.

JOHNNIE BAKER—Shooting at moving objects.

OUR INSULAR BROTHERS—Filipinos, Hawaiians, Cubans and Porto Ricans.

AMERICAN INDIANS—A Never-failing Subject of Interesting Study is our Red Brother, as he indulges in War Dances, Ghost Dances, Archery and Riding. The Attack on the Stage Coach by Savages.

Attacks on the SETTLER'S CABIN and the EMIGRANT TRAIN.
THE PONY EXPRESS—A Race Against Time in Conveying Mails Across the Trackless West.

SIXTH CAVALRY U. S. REGULARS

Garde-Kurassiers (German), Irish Fusiliers (Veterans of the Anglo-Boer War), U. S. Colored Infantry, A Battery of U. S. Regular Artillery and a Gattling Gun Brigade, showing sabre exercises, lance drill, tent pegging, cavalry maneuvers, artillery drill, (with loading and firing), accurate driving of cannon and caison.

NATE SALSBURY
VICE PREST
& MANAGER

GRAND STREET CAVALCADE ON THE MORNING OF EXHIBITION

PASSING THROUGH THE PRINCIPAL STREETS, LEAVING THE GROUNDS AT 9.30 O'CLOCK.

Two Performances Daily, Rain or Shine. Afternoon at 2 o'clock. Night at 8 o'clock. Doors Open One Hour Earlier.

ADMISSION, 50 Cents. CHILDREN UNDER NINE YEARS, HALF-PRICE. RESERVED SEATS, $1.00

RESERVED NUMBERED SEATS MAY BE SECURED DAY OF EXHIBITION AT

Layton & Neilson, Corner Sixth and Washington.

BY *1900 the Wild West had undergone a number of changes, which were reflected in the mode of dress worn by the cowboys. The earlier leather chaps were complemented by sheepskin. The latter style was featured in early western movies. (Courtesy Hastings Museum)*

and in 1900. The Boxer Rebellion of 1900 naturally triggered a new spectacle, an international one, as befitted the international operation that had been mounted to relieve Peking from the insurgent Boxers. The 1901 show displayed men in the uniforms of the allied expeditionary force, a veritable United Nations consisting of the United States and British Marines, Welsh Fusiliers, Germans, French, Russians, Japanese, and Sikhs. The new century also saw life-saving drill introduced. The Wild West was not exactly relegated to a sideline, but even with those eternal favorites, the Deadwood Stage, a buffalo hunt, and Pony Express riding, the emphasis had certainly changed. The ruggedness of touring re-mained, and so did the sheer logistics of the enterprise, not only the constant one-day stands but the fact that, as Cody reckoned, there were more than four thousand people in his employ.[52]

As if Cody and his executives had not enough to worry about, the show endured three train wrecks in less than two years. The last, near Louisville, North Car-olina, was the worst, with more than a hundred of the show's horses lost, includ-ing Cody's Old Pap. By some miracle, no one died. Reports that Annie Oakley was badly injured and hospitalized for a long spell have proved to be false. But she never again appeared with the Wild West. She and her beloved Frank died in 1926 within days of each other.[53]

But for Cody by far the worst blow—and one that was to be a great personal loss—was the death on Christmas Eve 1902 of Nate Salsbury, just before Cody started his last London engagement. The show opened as planned the day after Christmas. Every flag flew at half-mast, and the cavalry banner was draped in crepe. Wise, worldly, witty, and charm-ing, Salsbury was irreplaceable—and only time would tell just how much.[54]

NOTES

1 Nellie Snyder Yost, *Buffalo Bill: His Family, Friends, Failures, and Fortunes* (Chicago, 1979; hereafter cited as Yost, *Buffalo Bill*), 211.

2 Ibid., 211–219.

3 *Leavenworth Times,* January 29, 1889.

4 *Buffalo Bill's Wild West and Congress of Rough Riders of the World,* the offi-cial program for the 1892 season (hereafter cited as *Program, 1893*), 21–22; Glenn Shirley, *Pawnee Bill: A Biography of Major Gordon W. Lillie* (Albuquerque, 1958), 118–132; Don Russell, *The Lives and Legends of Buf-falo Bill* (Norman, Okla., 1960; here-after cited as Russell, *Lives*), 349–350.

5 Yost, *Buffalo Bill,* 221–222; Russell, *Lives,* 350.

6 John G. Neihardt (as told to), *Black Elk Speaks* (New York, 1932), 232; *Program, 1893,* 35; Carolyn Thomas Foreman, *Indians Abroad* (Norman, Okla., 1943), 203–204.

7 Yost, *Buffalo Bill,* 223.

8 *Program, 1893,* 59; Richard J. Walsh, with Milton S. Salsbury, *The Making of Buffalo Bill* (Indianapolis, 1928), 279.

9 *Program, 1893,* 29–30.

10 Ibid., 60; Time-Life Books, *The End and the Myth* (New York, 1979), 75.

11 Guiseppe Adami, ed., *Letters of Giacomo Puccini* (Philadelphia, 1931), 62.

12 *Program, 1893*, 60.

13 Russell, *Lives*, 353; An excellent resume of May's life is to be found in *The Reader's Encyclopedia of the American West*, 715–716.

14 L. G. Moses, "Wild West Shows, Reformers and the Image of the American Indian, 1887–1914," *South Dakota History* 4, no. 3 (Fall 1984; hereafter cited as Moses, "Wild West Shows"): 206.

15 Yost, *Buffalo Bill*, 224–225.

16 Moses, "Wild West Shows," 206.

17 Russell, *Lives*, 358.

18 Gen. Nelson A. Miles, *Serving the Republic* (Chicago and New York, 1896), 238.

19 James McLaughlin, *My Friend the Indian* (Boston, New York, and London, 1926), 179–222.

20 Russell, *Lives*, 360–361; Stanley Vestal, *Sitting Bull: Champion of the Sioux* (Norman, Okla., 1957; hereafter cited as Vestal, *Sitting Bull*), 287.

21 Russell, *Lives*, 361–363.

22 Vestal, *Sitting Bull*, 300–301.

23 Robert M. Utley, *Frontier Regulars* (New York, 1973), 403–408.

24 *Program, 1893*, 53.

25 Ibid., 50–51; Russell, *Lives*, 366–368.

26 Russell, *Lives*, 370.

27 *Program, 1893*, 54–55.

28 Russell, *Lives*, 371–372; Courtney Ryley Cooper, *Annie Oakley, Woman at Arms* (New York, 1927), 236.

29 Russell, *Lives*, 372; *Program, 1893*, 63–64.

30 Russell, *Lives*, 373.

31 Yost, *Buffalo Bill*, 227–255.

32 "Buffalo Bill in London," *Harper's Weekly*, September 3, 1892.

33 Queen Victoria's Journal, June 26, 1892, The Royal Archives, Windsor Castle, quoted by gracious permission of Her Majesty Queen Elizabeth II.

34 Nate Salsbury, "The Origin of the Wild West Show," *Colorado Magazine* 32, 3 (July 1955): 208–209.

35 Ibid., 210.

36 Ibid., 210–211.

37 Ibid., 211.

38 Russell, *Lives*, 374.

39 Yost, *Buffalo Bill*, 237; *Chicago Daily News*, June 26, 1893.

40 Yost, *Buffalo Bill*, 241; Russell, *Lives*, 375.

41 Yost, *Buffalo Bill*, 241–243.

42 *Itinerary of the Wild West*, The Buffalo Bill Historical Center, Cody, Wyoming (hereafter cited as *Itinerary*); Yost, *Buffalo Bill*, 243.

43 Russell, *Lives*, 378–379.

44 *Itinerary*; Russell, *Lives*, 379.

45 *Itinerary*; Ashland *Daily Press*, September 11, 1896.

46 *Itinerary* (Brooklyn and New York); Russell, *Lives*, 380–381.

47 Russell, *Lives*, 383–384.

48 Col. Tim McCoy and Ronald McCoy, *Tim McCoy Remembers the Wild West* (New York, 1977), 17.

49 Russell, *Lives*, 416–418; "Rare Recording by Buffalo Bill Is Given to Library of Congress," *Library of Congress Information Bulletin* 41, no. 11 (March 12, 1982): 77–78.

50 Yost, *Buffalo Bill*, 279–281.

51 Ibid., 281; *Itinerary*.

52 Russell, *Lives*, 419–420; Yost, *Buffalo Bill*, 299.

53 Yost, *Buffalo Bill*, 299.

54 Salsbury, "Origin of the Wild West Show," 204.

5

OLD SCOUTS NEVER DIE

The last European tour of the Wild West began in London on the day after Christmas 1902. It was at Earl's Court once again, and it received a big welcome. Business started to fall off, however, until a royal visit on March 14, 1903, gave it a boost. Along with King Edward VII and Queen Alexandra, the party included Prince Edward and Prince Albert, who would respectively become King Edward VIII and King George VI, both of whom, according to the *Daily Telegraph*, were "evidently keenly interested at the prospect of seeing Buffalo Bill." The audience, not having expected royalty, was thrilled by the added sense of occasion. Cody, on a black charger, announced, "Your Majesties, ladies and gentlemen, allow me to introduce to you the greatest Congress of Rough Riders in the World." The king raised his hat, and the young princes, unable to sit down in their excitement, looked delighted as the hero of the hour came close to them. There was not, said the reporter, a dull moment. Perish the thought.[1]

The princes liked the cowboys best, and after the show the king especially asked to see Johnny Baker. He told Baker that he was glad to see him again, and he recalled his performance in the first London show. Baker shook the king's hand vigorously and later said that the way he had been talked to was "simply lovely," adding that he had been called a wonderful shot. Another high spot that the princes enjoyed was the visit to the

MAJOR-General Robert Baden-Powell, hero of the siege of Mafeking in the Boer War, photographed in 1907 at the first Boy Scout camp. The distinctive wide-brimmed hat later worn by the Boy Scouts owes its origin more to the North-West Mounted Police and the type of hat worn in South Africa than it does to Buffalo Bill's sombrero. Buffalo Bill himself was a great admirer of Baden-Powell and his scouts, and Cody's interest contributed to the formation of a similar organization in the United States. (Courtesy the Librarian, Baden-Powell House, London)

Indian village. Said Cody, "I have never seen children more delighted than the little princes were. It was a joy to see and hear them." He added that he was returning after this season and was particularly gratified to see the king and queen and the American ambassador and Mrs. Choate. "Altogether it has been a record day for us," he said. By now ambassadors had to take Cody very seriously, for he was surely one of the finest ambassadors the United States has ever had.[2]

The show moved to Manchester, where it opened on April 13, 1903. Unfortunately, it was a black day for Cody and his public, for as he was leaving the arena his horse shied at some shifting scenery and reared up and fell back. Cody could not quite clear himself, so one of his legs was injured. However, at the evening performance and later ones he rode around the arena in an open carriage, to

Buffalo Bill's Saddle,

M. DOROTHY *Hardy, a noted artist in the early years of this century, received Cody's permission to sketch the members of the Wild West. This drawing of his saddle is one of many she made in 1904. (Courtesy the late Edward Blackmore)* ABOVE

WHEN M. *Dorothy Hardy died in 1939, this saddle (which she had purchased from a member of the Wild West) stood in her studio, and astride it was a figure dressed in cowboy clothing. Edward Blackmore acquired this and other items from her collection and used the saddle for some years. It is still in good condition, but some years ago its sheepskin lining had to be destroyed. Made in the 1870s by L. D. Stone of San Francisco, it is a double cinch (or rimfire) version and has no side jockeys. (From the collection of Joseph G. Rosa)* OPPOSITE

the delight of the crowds. The Battle of San Juan Hill was a particular success on this tour, and the Indians—Arapahoes, Brulé Sioux and Cheyennes—were another major attraction. Powerful arc lamps lit the evening performances at Manchester and, so one paper stated,

"considering the arctic weather the attendances have been surprisingly good." As far as one reporter was concerned, despite the absence of Cody, the show "as a thrilling and realistic exhibition has surely never been surpassed."[3]

From then on, the tour consisted mainly of one-night stands with longer stays in major cities such as Liverpool, Leeds, and Cardiff. Long before the coauthor's town of Wimbledon was visited on June 18, 1904, Cody was back in action. The local Wimbledon reporter noted one feature that indicates the way the show added attractions steadily down the years—without removing the magical standard items—for one "Carter the cowboy cyclist in his wonderful bicycle leap through space, across a chasm of 56 feet" covered a "distance in the plunge of 151 feet." Veterans of the U.S. Artillery, the Sixth U.S. Cavalry, and veteran British cavalrymen were also in the show.[4]

Cody had gone home early the pre-

THIS *fine portrait of Buffalo Bill garbed in a manner that had almost become his personal trademark was published in the* Illustrated and Dramatic News, London, *on March 14, 1903. (From the collection of Robin May)*

vious winter. The 1903 season ended at Burton-on-Trent after weather that appalled him—fifty hours of steady rain "and the worst wind storms" he had ever experienced. A show had had to be cancelled, which was just as well, since a house collapsed, and the debris fell where members of the public would have been sitting.[5]

The seasons of 1903 and 1904 in Britain were hugely successful financially. Winter quarters were at Stoke-on-Trent each year. The last town to see Buffalo Bill was the neighboring one of Hanley, on October 10, 1904. The company was better off than its chief, for, as will be seen, early in 1905 he was in the midst of his divorce hearing. When the company visited France in the spring, Paris provided huge crowds. Johnny Baker was now a famous shot and also equestrian director of the show. Iron Tail was the leader of the Indian contingent and would remain so until the end. In fact, the end of the glory days had come, though the show would survive, despite crises and changes, for another decade. Cody beat off competition from J. T. McCaddon's International Shows—which included a Wild West—so successfully that the interloper fled across the Chan-

nel just ahead of a posse of creditors. Far more serious, however, was an outbreak of glanders, which resulted in two hundred out of three hundred of Cody's horses having to be destroyed. A shattering blow to both morale and finances, it was followed by the sudden death of James Bailey early in 1906. A note for $12,000 was discovered. It dated back to happier days in London and had Cody's signature on it. As Don Russell has written, if Cody said he had paid it, then he had. Yet it was another blow. Dreams of retirement were banished. Debts, plus the fact that Bailey's wife and other heirs to his estate wanted to leave show business, meant that Cody could not afford to leave.[6]

Gloom must surely have been banished, however, for business in France and Italy was brisk. We find Cody helping victims of both the eruption of Vesuvius and the San Francisco earthquake. In 1906 the company visited Austria, Germany, Hungary, Luxembourg, and Belgium—also Russia briefly—during a season that ended in Arles, France, on October 30. The magic of the Wild West remained potent—as did the star himself. As soon as he returned to New York he got down to planning the next show and, with a blessed reaction against too many nonwestern acts, he added a new western item, the Battle of Summit Springs (1869). He asked General Carr and others for their memories, and, of course, he could use his own. He also had a Union Pacific train hold-up with "Bandit Hun-

THIS original James E. Hunt photograph personally autographed by Buffalo Bill was found in an Eastbourne, Sussex, junk store by the late Edward Blackmore. He kept it for a number of years before presenting it to Joseph G. Rosa, together with the Western stock saddle once owned by the late M. Dor- othy Hardy. Hunt photographed the Wild West on a number of occasions between 1903 and 1904 and perhaps earlier. This portrait of Cody mounted on the "black charger" that he rode during most of the tour is considered one of his finest. (From the col- lection of Joseph G. Rosa)

THESE *Sioux Indians were photographed at Land's End, Cornwall, England, ca. 1904. Even today, the appearance of American Indians at Land's End would arouse much in-* *terest. The lone cowboy has not been iden- tified. (Courtesy Buffalo Bill Historical Cen- ter)*

ters" arriving in the nick of time. Madison Square Garden, scene of former Cody triumphs, saw this excellently per- formed attraction in 1907. It toured two years, doubtless gladdening many thou- sands of hearts, for it was a stunning act both theatrically and mechanically.[7]

Cody was now entirely responsible for his own show and would be for two years. True, he owned only a third of it, and that third was mortgaged. Considering

the complexity of the situation, Bailey's heirs and the Salsbury share and Cody managed well enough. The heirs had es- tablished the Bailey Estate Trust, and in 1906 they sold the Bailey interest in Adam Forepaugh and Sells Brothers to Ringling Brothers, who were the co- owners. The Ringlings followed this up by acquiring the ailing Barnum and Bailey show, now a shadow of its former self.[8]

The Bailey estate, meanwhile, suggested that Gordon Lillie might merge his Pawnee Bill show with that of Cody, whose own position was not helped by the argument about whether he had paid the note mentioned earlier. As for Lillie, his recent career had been erratic but lively, both at home and in Europe. His shows had included Pawnee Bill's Historic Far West and Great Far East. In 1908 Lillie suggested that he and Cody should join forces, but the merger failed because Cody understandably did not want to share billing with him. However, after more crises, the two did join forces, combining Buffalo Bill's Wild West with Pawnee Bill's Great Far East, shortened by employees to the "Two Bills Show." Pawnee Bill thought big, so big that his vast scenic effects designed for Madison Square Garden could not allow the Deadwood Stage and other vital pieces to get into the arena. Tantrums were the order of the day, with Johnny Baker, the arena director, in a sullen mood and with Cody allegedly driven to tears. Nevertheless, the first night, complete with the governors of New York and New Jersey and Cody's good friend General Miles in the front, was a triumph.[9]

Enter the badmen in the shape of the heirs of the deceased Bailey. Lillie was told to sack John Burke and general manager Cooke. In-fighting was brisk, but Lillie came out on top, not least because he got Cody's disputed note cancelled. He was now in charge, but he insisted that Cody be co-owner. Unlike the majority of the businessmen they had to deal with, Lillie understood the power of the name Buffalo Bill. The show was an extraordinary mixture of acts. The Great Far East did not, as the billboards suggested, hog half the show, being a single, circus-like salute to the Orient. This "dream of the Orient" included Japanese, Arabs, Russians, Singhalese, a Hindu fakir, Moors, South Sea Islanders, Syrians, Australian boomerang throwers, and musical elephants. Old Wild West favorites and the more recent Battle of Summit Springs were on the bill, as was Football on Horseback, an Indian-versus-Cowboys romp with few rules and plenty of audience appeal. Happily, the truly western flavor was much as before, with the Great Train Hold-Up now firmly established. The show had veered towards the circus though, including clowns and an elephant.[10]

Cody, who had half-wanted to retire for a long time, could not afford to do so, but he had set his sights on retiring in 1910, and the public knew it. Pawnee Bill would take over in the arena and in dime novels. The magic date was chosen because he would be sixty-four then, when "all my old Army friends retire." Of course, he had had and would continue to have other plans, which would rarely succeed and which will be noted later. The retirement would be postponed, but he meant it to be final that night in Madison Square Garden in 1910. There

BUFFALO *Bill at the wheel of an "Atlas" automobile ca. 1907. He was happy to be photographed sitting in or driving a car, but when it was suggested that he drive one into the arena at the commencement of perfor-* *mances, he was appalled. It would be left to Hollywood in later years to introduce cars and airplanes into its own unique version of the "Wild West." (Courtesy Melvin A. Schulte)*

would later be many permutations of the speech that the audience heard on May 14, 1910:

> I am about to go home for a well-earned rest. Out in the West I have my horses, my buffaloes, my sturdy, staunch old Indian friends—my home and my green fields, but I never see them green. When my season is over the hillsides and the meadows have been blighted by a wintry frost and the sere and yellow leaves cover the ground. I want to see nature in its prime, to enjoy a rest from active life. My message to you to-night is one of farewell. Thirty years ago you gave me my first welcome here. I am grateful

IT *could be said that Buffalo Bill's Wild West knew no bounds, and this photograph taken at the State Penitentiary, Auburn, New York, on July 30, 1908, is a poignant reminder that the "freedom of the West and* *the open plains" could mean many things to many people. Notice the discreet placement of the prison guards. (Courtesy Buffalo Bill Historical Center)*

for your continued loyal devotion to me. During that time many of my friends among you and many of those with me have been long since gathered to the great unknown arena of another life—there are only a few of us left. When I went away from here each year before I merely said good night— this time it will mean goodbye. To my little friends in the gallery and the grown-ups who used to sit there, I thank you once again. God bless you all—goodbye.[11]

In September the North Platte *Telegraph* reprinted this speech with this addition: "It is my purpose to leave the active management of the exhibits I have created in the hands of my partner, Major G. W. Lillie, 'Pawnee Bill' . . . who will

JOSEPH E. Stimson, a Cheyenne, Wyoming, photographer, made a large number of eight-by-ten-inch glass plates of Cody's Wild West. His own record indicates that they were taken at Omaha, Nebraska, in 1907, but the Wild West did not appear there that year. Omaha welcomed Cody in August 1908 and September 1909, and this view, together with the illustrations that follow, of the grand entry was made in one of those months. The large glass plates enabled Stimson to produce some impressive enlargements with no distortion. It is also evident that he had several cameras in operation at the same time to record sequences in quick succession. (Courtesy Wyoming State Archives)

continue the enterprise . . . but without my presence in the saddle." We are told that at the end of Cody's speech there was not a dry eye in Madison Square Garden.[12]

It had been a fine season, with a profit of $400,000. Unfortunately, much of the revenue would be lost in Cody's Arizona mine, the Oracle. That the show's organization and morale were still superb was conclusively proved on May 24, 1911. It was due to play Lowell, Massachusetts, that day but a train wreck occurred near the town. The company rapidly rounded

MR. Stimson must have tripped his camera shutters at great speed to obtain pictures of the Pony Express. In earlier views, the rider leaps for the horse to the right of the photograph and is handed his "mochilla" by the central figure, who brandishes a Winchester rifle. (Courtesy Wyoming State Archives) TOP

MILITARY riders representing several nations performing in the arena for the Omaha crowd. (Courtesy Wyoming State Archives) ABOVE

ARABIAN acrobats go through their paces in between the gunsmoke and gallop. (Courtesy Wyoming State Archives) OPPOSITE, TOP

FROM *left to right: unidentified cowboy, Iron Tail, Irma Cody, Buffalo Bill, and, mounted on a horse, William Cody Boal,* *son of Cody's eldest daughter, Arta. (Courtesy Wyoming State Archives)*

THIS *photograph of buffalo taken by Stimson at Omaha seems particularly fetching—at least one animal is "wallowing" in public* *acclaim! (Courtesy Wyoming State Archives)*

up the animals, managed the expected town parade, and opened on time that afternoon. Cody, Johnny Baker, and the rest of the company had worked miracles. However, the tour—of New England, the Midwest, Nebraska, Kansas, Colorado, and the South—was not a financial success, and Cody was unwell for some of the time. Final engagements included a triumphant one at North Platte. The farewell speech was regularly delivered, a consummation devoutly to be wished but not yet possible. Cody asked Lillie if he would buy Scout's Rest for $100,000. Of this, $80,000 went to his wife and the rest to Lillie, to whom Cody owed $30,000. A $10,000 mortgage on the Irma Hotel at Cody, Wyoming—named in 1902 for his daughter—was transferred to Lillie. The 1911 deal left Cody half-owner of the show, while his mine in Arizona was selling tungsten ore. Yet despite a profit for the year, the Arizona mine was too costly to run, so when Cody did actually retire at the close of the season in Columbia, South Carolina, in October 1912, he found that his retirement would be short.[13]

Cody's business ventures must now be examined more closely. From the 1890s

THE *Deadwood Stage at Omaha. Still pulled by six mules, the most famous of western conveyances—a version of the cele-* *brated Concord coach—pauses between acts. (Courtesy Wyoming State Archives)*

until his death, the name of Buffalo Bill Cody was linked with a number of schemes, some of which were complete failures, others of which were moderately or even very successful. When General Sheridan retained Cody at Fort McPherson in 1871 and allowed the Fifth Cavalry to go to Arizona without him, there were, as we have noted, other compensa-

tions. Twenty years later, however, Cody made the first of many visits to Arizona. In November 1892, he and some friends started on a trek (a large part of it on horseback) from Scout's Rest to the Grand Canyon and other parts of the state. At Flagstaff the local press noted that the party had "had a pleasant trip across country and speak in highest terms

CHIEF *Iron Tail (minus war bonnet) sits among fellow Sioux, who have not been identified. (Courtesy Wyoming State Ar- chives, Museums and Historical Depart- ment)*

of the courtesy extended to them along the way. They are here to hunt bear, deer, and other game, and to study the flora, fauna, and geological formations. Some of the company are of a scientific mind."[14]

Cody's exploration extended as far as Utah, but it was in Arizona that his real interest lay. At Camp Bonito, some forty- two miles northeast of Tucson and close to Oracle, in partnership with Colonel

D. B. Dyer, a former Indian agent, he es- tablished the Cody-Dyer Mining and Milling Company. It was never a prof- itable venture. Cody poured more money into it than he ever got out in ores, but he enjoyed the experience, and the local people liked him.

In 1895, Cody joined George T. Beck and others to form the Cody Canal Proj- ect, a scheme undertaken by the Sho- shone Land and Irrigation Company in

STIMSON'S *photographs are particularly valuable in conveying the size of the arena at Omaha. Obviously, the size was dictated by the location, but it is clear that no space was wasted. Here the Battle of Summit Springs is being re-enacted. Two white female "captives" can clearly be seen in the foreground. (Courtesy Wyoming State Archives, Museums and Historical Department)*

the Big Horn Mountain region of Wyoming. Attempts to name the townsite laid out by the company Shoshone were rejected by the post office, who thought it would be confused with the Shoshone Indian Agency. Instead, they called the place Cody, the name it still bears, and it is there that the museum and historical center are now located. Unlike the mines

at Camp Bonito, the irrigation scheme paid off. The Shoshone Dam was completed in 1910 and was then called the highest in the world, some 328 feet. In 1946 it was renamed the Buffalo Bill Dam.[15]

Scout's Rest had been designed as a haven for Cody, but his constant bickering with Louisa led him to move most of

THE *close of the Battle of Summit Springs. Colonel Cody takes a shot at departing warriors as his troops "rescue" the white captives. (Courtesy Wyoming State Archives, Museums and Historical Department)* OPPOSITE, TOP

ADVANCING *years did not prevent Buffalo Bill from sharpshooting at glass balls tossed into the air. Isham, his horse, seems to be content to come along for the ride. (Courtesy Wyoming State Archives, Museums and Historical Department)* OPPOSITE, BOTTOM

his cattle to Wyoming by 1895. He also acquired his friend Mike K. Russell's "TE" Brand Ranch. By the early years of this century, Cody's famous TE Ranch covered more than forty-six hundred acres of the Big Horn Basin holdings.[16]

By 1905, relations between Cody and his wife had reached the breaking point. The strain was exacerbated by the death of their daughter Arta on January 30. Arta's first husband, Horton Boal, had died on January 1, 1902, and she later married Dr. Charles W. Thorp. Arta died in Spokane, Washington, but it was decided she should be buried beside Kit and Orra in Rochester, New York. Cody telegraphed his wife and sought her agreement to forget past differences. Instead, claiming that Cody had broken Arta's heart, Louisa Cody blamed him for Arta's death. Arta had tended to side with her mother against Cody when he and Lulu disagreed, and there must have been

times when the aging scout wondered just who was on his side. No matter what he did, it seemed, he encountered prejudice when he looked for praise. Even at Arta's funeral, Lulu could not put aside her wrath; she made a scene in a Chicago hotel, denouncing Buffalo Bill and his sisters, with whom she had frequently crossed swords. So it was no surprise when, in February–March 1905, the long-expected divorce action took place.[17]

The preliminaries to the action had been dragged around various Wyoming courts for several years, during which time depositions had been taken on both sides. To avoid conflict (both parties had many friends in the area), Judge Charles Scott, who was neutral and prepared to hear the evidence, was brought up from Cheyenne.

Mrs. John Boyer, wife of the superintendent of Scout's Rest Ranch, declared that Mrs. Cody had laced her husband's coffee with a drug called Dragon's Blood. Mrs. Boyer, however, switched cups and for some extraordinary reason drank the coffee intended for the colonel. She became violently sick. She was quick to point out, however, that she did not think Louisa intended her husband any harm. Rather, she just wanted some kind of hold over him. Under cross-examination she admitted that there was bad feeling between herself and Mrs. Cody, who had once accused her of keeping a girl for Mr. Boyer's use. Mrs. Boyer also admitted

LOUISA *Cody, photographed ca. 1888 or 1889. (Courtesy Scout's Rest Ranch)*

that following a row with Mrs. Cody, she had grabbed her by the throat and thrown her out of the house.

Testifying on March 6, which he admitted was his thirty-ninth wedding anniversary, Cody recalled his youthful gullibility, saying that he had agreed to the engagement as a joke and had not realized that Louisa had taken him seriously. Her letters reminded him of his promise and, prompted by what he described as "keeping my word," he agreed to the marriage.

Cody said that their first separation had come in 1877. In the box he proved to be a bad witness. He stated that at the end of the season, it was customary for the ladies in the cast of his theatrical dramas to drink a few beers, and in high spirits they would say: "Papa, we want to kiss you good bye." Cody had no objection, but his wife, who on one occasion was in another room and heard the jollity, was enraged—her anger still burned thirty years later. Cody found this difficult to understand, but when one reads his floundering explanation of the often broadminded reaction of actresses to any kind of relationship, one can better appreciate how Lulu, brought up in a staid and Victorian religious background, must have felt.

Louisa alleged that Cody was frequently drunk but admitted that she, too, drank and occasionally became quarrelsome. She also made it clear that she resented the attention paid to Cody by

Queen Victoria and later by Queen Alexandra. Although these feelings were dismissed as nonsense and discredited many of Louisa's allegations against other women in her husband's life, they helped to explain how she sometimes became violent. The episode of Cody's association with Katherine Clemmons (or Olive Clemons) in Chicago, when Louisa discovered them and started to break up the place, was exhumed at the trial. The judge, however, ordered some allegations to be struck from the record.

Speculation about Cody's romantic associations with actresses and others remains rife. His divorce action had laid several charges at his door, but nothing was ever proved. Judge Scott found in favor of Mrs. Cody, stating that "all the allegations in the amended answers of the said defendant, Louisa Cody, are true, and that the allegations of the plaintiff's petition and amended petition and any supplemental petition are hereby disproved." Cody not only lost the suit, but he had to pay his wife's costs, which amounted to $318.[18]

The rift between Cody and Louisa lasted until July 28, 1910, when the Wild West was playing at North Platte. Despite their stormy differences, she had never deviated from her belief that "Will is one of the kindest and most generous of men." The family persuaded them to meet and then left them alone. When they emerged, they had agreed to carry on as before. Lulu was even persuaded to join Cody at Camp Bonito, where he had built the Mountain View Hotel. While he was with the Wild West or inspecting his various enterprises, she was happy to sit knitting on the veranda for months at a time.[19]

But if Buffalo Bill the man had his faults—as every man has—in the eyes of his greatest fans, the children, he could do no wrong. He loved them and they loved him. Once, when asked by a cousin if she could bring some children to one of his performances at Ambrose Park, Brooklyn, he replied: "I love children; bring them all." His own children found him to be a loving, caring father. This attitude was reflected in his reaction to the thousands who came to see the Wild West. The hero of the dime novel was there in the flesh. Less than a generation later Buffalo Bill's Wild West would be reenacted in countless motion pictures to reach an audience far greater than he could have imagined, but for his young audiences the effect was always the same—it was magic.[20]

Sadly, Cody's last years were not much touched with magic. In November 1912, he went to Denver to see his sister May. His costly Arizona mine had still not produced enough to allow him to leave show business. For the past three years his share of the "Two Bills Show" had helped run his mines and pay his personal debts. Lillie kept the show's winter quarters going and took Cody's share of the winter's costs from their company's earnings

SOME *versions of this photograph have been dated as early as 1889, but in view of Cody's white hair and goatee we think that it is ca. 1914. The location, however, is still subject to conjecture. (Courtesy Kansas State Historical Society)* ABOVE

WILLIAM *Mathewson in later years. Known as early as 1860 as Buffalo Bill, Mathewson is believed to be the original Kansas "Buffalo Bill." There were, of course, other "Buffalo Bills" in the Old West, but it was Cody who became immortalized as the Buffalo Bill. (Courtesy Kansas State Historical Society)* OPPOSITE

each spring. However, as has been seen, 1911 was an unfortunate season, and Lillie asked Cody to put up his share to $20,000. Only then would it take the road in the spring. This was the other reason for his trip to Denver, where he had the misfortune to fall in with two unsavory characters, Harry H. Tammen and Frederick G. Bonfils.[21]

There was a certain awful charm about these two rogues, who had bought the *Denver Post* in 1894 and made it a colossal, if lurid, success. They had come up via bartending, Bonfils later providing the main financial stimulus, after having made a goodly sum from an illicit lottery in Chicago. Tammen was born in Baltimore. Gene Fowler, a brilliant journalist who chronicled their rise to infamy, undoubtedly liked Cody and respected his military record, but he was out to entertain. Fowler's portrait of Cody as a drunkard is hardly consistent with the record of a showman who almost never missed a performance—Fowler's Cody would have missed dozens! As for the new owners of the *Evening Post* (as the *Denver Post* was called for a time), they started "crusading" away against every possible target. It was "The Paper with a Heart and a Soul" and, said its many enemies, "a Price!"[22]

Always on the look-out for new interests, Tammen, with no encouragement from Bonfils, decided on show business, starting off modestly by purchasing a dog and pony show, the Floto Dog and Pony Company, its name taken from his sports

editor, Otto Floto, because of its sound. Floto grew, and now Bonfils was interested. Dogs and ponies were no longer the only animals, and soon the Ringlings had to take note. The show became the Sells-Floto Circus because "Sells," too, sounded right—the Sells Brothers were leaders in the spangles world and their name was bought. Pictures of Floto and all four Sells Brothers appeared on the show's posters and bills. After much infighting in the hothouse world of the circus, William Sells was legally allowed to stay on the billboards, but portraits of his brothers were banished. It was a costly partial victory, but that did not deter the Denver duo, who would soon have Cody in their clutches.[23]

The Ringling Brothers were kept out of Denver by Tammen's influence over the mayor, and it was now that he and Bonfils aspired to swallowing Buffalo Bill's Wild West and Pawnee Bill's Far East. Cody was in trouble because the Oracle mine was not producing enough gold or tungsten. Retirement was still a dream, for there were still too many debts to pay. It cost $40,000 to house the show through the winter. Lillie asked if Cody could raise $20,000 to help cope with the winter's costs. Fate found Cody in Denver visiting his sister, Mrs. May Decker, and during this visit he met Tammen and Bonfils. His problems, he believed, were at once solved, for Tammen was only too ready to lend him the $20,000 for six months at six percent.[24]

CODY *may have purchased this coach in England and had it shipped to North Platte, or it might have been made by Abbott & Downing of Concord, New Hampshire, makers of the celebrated Concord coaches, of* *which the Deadwood Stage was an excellent example. In any event, the coach resembles the famous English coaches beloved of Christmas card artists. (Courtesy Scout's Rest Ranch)*

The *Post* gloatingly reported:

The most important deal ever consummated in American amusement enterprise was closed in Denver a few days ago, when Colonel W. F. Cody (Buffalo Bill) put his name to a contract with the proprietors of the Sells-Floto Circus, the gist of which is that these two big shows consolidate in its entirety, and the "Buffalo Bill Exposition of Frontier Days and the Passing of the West" with the historic incidents associated with them, shall also be preserved, added to, and given with the circus performance.

This means, not only from a showman's, but a layman's standpoint, the strongest combination ever formed in the history of American amusements, if not in the world.

This departure marks the culmination of many years' hard work by the Sells-Floto people. The circus is now in its twelfth year, and during that time has been made the target for more opposition and battling in various ways than any organization that ever went on the road. Everyone conversant with the history of the show business remembers the fights with the Ringling Brothers, Barnum and Bailey Circus and other attractions which combined in what is commonly known as "the circus trust." For many seasons the smaller circuses went up and down the country losing money in many thousands, but ever since they instituted the cut-rate price, their rivals have been more than willing to make way for them and to prefer their room rather than their company. The present combination would seem to make the Sells-Floto Shows the monarchs of the amusement field.[25]

Apart from the initial contradiction that the two shows were and were not now one, Tammen was surely stating that Cody was now his man, even if he was not claiming the famous old title, Buffalo Bill's Wild West. It certainly seemed that Cody had abandoned his share in his own show in exchange for Tammen's loan. Whether he could legally do so was another matter, for Lillie, with the threat of foreclosure hanging over him because of an old and forgotten debt of his partner's, had incorporated the show in New Jersey. Cody telegraphed a confused Lillie, telling him to pay no attention to the press. "I have done nothing that will interfere with our show," he confidently and sincerely stated. "The confused Colonel," as Gene Fowler calls him at this point, can

BUFFALO *Bill ca. 1911 at about the time he met his namesake, William ("Buffalo Bill") Mathewson, at Wichita. Fortunately for posterity neither gentleman thought their disagreement over title claims merited a duel! (Courtesy Scout's Rest Ranch)*

be guilty only of confusion. Russell, aware of Cody's desire to retire, thought it unlikely that Cody would knowingly sign such an agreement unless he believed that it would be canceled when the loan was repaid. Perhaps Cody had not read the agreement before he signed it, in the mistaken belief that he had signed another note or mortgage. Why else, asks one expert, "would he publicly reassure the press and Pawnee Bill?"[26]

Poor Pawnee Bill could only believe that he had been double-crossed by his partner, who would soon be with Tammen, so he naturally no longer concerned himself with Cody's debts; the show had been incorporated. Tammen had no immediate reason to rejoice, for the elements sabotaged the show. After a New York engagement the unlucky company hit wretched weather—floods and bitter cold—as they headed through the South, a South hit by a fall in the price of cotton. Cody became ill at Knoxville on June 6, while business was atrocious; a hundred successive stands lost money. The Indians understandably had had enough, and many deserted. Pine Ridge supplied some more, but there would be no work for them.[27]

Worse was to come. After performing in Illinois, Iowa, and Nebraska early in July, the company was due to appear in Denver on the twenty-first, within days of the due date on the note that Cody had signed six months earlier. Lillie was now so hostile to Cody that he was not in the least concerned about the consequences. Yet he was warned by a friend who worked in the United States Printing and Lithographic Company—controlled by Tammen—of the huge printing debt that was owed for the show's publicity posters, programs, etc. The note, which included 1912 dues, was for more than $60,000, and though Lillie did not realize it, Tammen was happy to ruin the show. What he wanted was the name and the person of Buffalo Bill Cody.[28]

The result was the wrong sort of high drama on the lot, with the sheriff's men heading for the treasury wagon. Cody spotted them and ordered Thomas A. Smith to grab the day's takings, but the sheriff beat him to it. Cody was devastated, for he was unable to pay his employees and feed them or the animals. Even the company's belongings had been seized. His distraught colleagues simply had the clothes they were wearing. Of course, Lillie could have saved the show with his own money, but he was far too angry to do so. He knew that Cody would be part of Sells-Floto the following season. To file a bankruptcy petition, he sped to New Jersey, where the show had been incorporated. Before he was able to file his own claim he was faced with an involuntary petition of bankruptcy against the Buffalo Bill Wild West and Pawnee Bill Far East.[29]

Lillie's bitterness did him no good. Adolph Marks, the general counsel for the lithograph company, was highly critical of Lillie and refused to allow any blame to be attached to Cody for the sequence of events. He knew that Cody's position was impossible because he had deeded to Lillie his only negotiable properties, the North Platte Ranch and the Irma Hotel, worth $100,000 and $75,000 respectively. Cody had been willing to transfer both deeds to the lithograph company, but Lillie's judgment was totally astray by this time. In fact, the show had taken some $30,000, but Lillie had failed to pay a promised $10,000, let alone any of the printing bills. In Denver, Lillie asked for a day's delay after admitting his default, but this was refused. However, Marks offered to delay collection of account for two years providing that Lillie agreed to transfer the mortgages on the Cody real estate to his company. Lillie would have none of it. A somewhat bewildered Cody now found himself having to sue Lillie to force him to account for monies received. With Tammen attaching the show for Cody's $20,000 note, Pawnee Bill was beaten and indeed finished with show business, even though he retained much of his own money.[30]

Cody did his best to help his people, most of whom were stranded so far from home. At one stage people and animals were sleeping together. On September 15

BUFFALO *Bill mounted on Isham at his TE Ranch, ca. 1912. This magnificent animal carried Cody around the arena for some years and was a great favorite with the crowds. Isham presaged the white-horse image later popularized by Buck Jones's "Silver," Ken Maynard's "Tarzan," and others.*

In 1913, when the Wild West went under the hammer, many considered Isham to be an old nag, but Colonel C. J. Bills from Lincoln, Nebraska, pushed up the bidding to $150 and presented the old warrior to Cody as a gift. Buffalo Bill was tearfully overjoyed. (Courtesy Scout's Rest Ranch)

came the bitter day of the auction of the show. Two friends saw to it that Cody's horse Isham fetched a good price and got back to its owner. Some Boy Scouts who had been with the show since Chicago marched back via North Platte.[31]

Cody would say that Tammen had bro-

ken his heart, but the grand old trouper was anything but finished. London again beckoned; a variety theater offered him $2,500. He demanded twice as much, but his demand was rejected. Then his life brightened up. Tammen suggested that he appear in motion pictures. His mind gradually conceived a splendid series of grand historical films, and Tammen and Bonfils, not surprisingly, agreed. So did the secretary of war and General Miles. Troops would be provided, Pine Ridge would be used for locations, and, of course, the resident Indians would be available. The Essanay Company of Chicago would make the films for the Colonel W. F. Cody (Buffalo Bill) Historical Picture Company.[32]

It was a decade since Gilbert M. ("Bronco Bill") Anderson appeared in *The Great Train Robbery* (filmed in the wilds of New Jersey in 1903), and for the first time a motion picture told a story. Now, "the greatest film ever made, a lasting pictorial history of those early campaigns to hand down to posterity" was to be made—in Wyoming. Real cowboys and Indians, Indians who had actually fought the white men, were to be used, Johnny Baker would direct, Cody would kill Yellow Hand once again—a remarkable feat at his age—but so what? It was a new extension of the old Wild West. Realism obtruded via General Miles, who demanded and apparently got six hundred cavalrymen to march past the camera time and again so that his eleven-thousand-strong 1891 army might be seen. Presumably no one dared to point out the absurdity of such a happening, though it seems that some of the time no film was actually turning![33]

Cody was back in action in 1914— back with Tammen—in "Sells-Floto

THE *snake and the rabbit. Harry H. Tammen eyes Buffalo Bill in this photograph, ca. 1913. Their relationship was never a happy one. Cody's appearance with the 101 Ranch Show soon made him tired and affected his health. On October 14, 1916, he wrote to his friend Henry J. Hersey at Denver that he hoped his health would soon improve as "I have got a treatment that's positively making a well man of me. My courage and ambition is returning, and I am going to fly at it and make another fortune. Can Tammen block me?" By the thirtieth, however, he told his friend that he was worn out. Tammen, he wrote, had a contract with Edward Arlington "for my birthright at $25 a day and Nov. 11th his company will have paid Tammen $4,500 for my services for this season." Cody also declared that Tammen owed him $11,000. (Extracts from the Cody-Hersey correspondence kindly supplied by Melvin A. Schulte, who owns the original letters.) (Courtesy Buffalo Bill Historical Center)*

Circus and Buffalo Bill's Wild West— Two Big Institutions joined together at one Price of Admission," which was twenty-five cents. Cody appeared in the saddle and introduced each performance but no longer shot or took part in any of the show's acts. He was well paid at $1,000 plus forty percent of receipts above $3,000. He never ceased to meet influential people and generally publicize the show. The Oracle mine was never forgotten, and Johnny Baker, in England to take part in the shooting at the 1914 An-

A GLIMPSE of the filming of a re-enactment of Wounded Knee in 1913. Left to right: Cody, General Miles, Johnny Baker, and Colonel Marion Maus. The Sioux Indian has not been identified. (Courtesy South Dakota State Historical Society)

GENERAL Nelson A. Miles was persuaded to join Buffalo Bill when Cody announced his intention to film a re-enactment of several Indian war battles. It is claimed that for the sake of authenticity, Miles demanded that six hundred cavalrymen trot past the cameras until the eleven thousand men of his 1891 command were recorded. What he did not know, apparently, was that for most of the time the turning cameras had no film in them! (Courtesy Kansas State Historical Society) OPPOSITE

THE *elderly gentleman with Buffalo Bill has not been identified, but behind Cody can be seen an advertisement for his film on the In-* *dian war, complete copies of which are unknown today. (Courtesy Buffalo Bill Historical Center)*

glo-American Exhibition, did his best to find investors for the Oracle and to interest the British in Cody's films. The season left Cody exhausted and ill, but visits to his sister in Denver and his TE Ranch restored him. He was especially pleased when he killed a big buck deer by moonlight. The Cody Club of Wyoming gave him a grand sixty-ninth birthday party on February 26, 1915.[34]

Meanwhile, in Denver while Cody was sick, Tammen talked him into another season. Cody was still not reading contracts properly and did not notice that he would be getting forty percent for receipts above $3,100 instead of the previous season's $3,000. Clearly such little victories delighted the soul of the mighty Tammen. Cody still looked superb and was able to continue the tours he had undertaken for so long. The old spirit was there. When Tammen made outrageous claims about what Cody allegedly owed him, he came to see Cody in Lawrence, Kansas. The old scout wrote a friend that though he had avoided killing in the bad old days, he was prepared to kill Tammen. The wretched visitor was afraid to enter the tent until Cody assured him that he would be safe. The result was that Cody agreed to stay till the end of the 1915 season. At the end of the season Cody was able to boast that he had not missed a single show—366 of them in 183 days—despite much bad weather. He was speaking at the annual farewell dinner on October 14, 1915, held that year at Fort Worth just before the end of the season.[35]

Buffalo Bill was as fine a leader as ever. At Fort Madison, Iowa, the previous August the show was situated near a swamp, which flooded in a storm. Of the circus staff of four hundred, only six—including Cody—stayed to carry the children and help the women to safety.[36]

In February 1916, Cody was touring and lecturing with his films, finishing in New York City. Tammen had hoped to get a percentage out of the tour, but George K. Spoor of Essanay managed to prevent that from happening. However, Cody's desire to have Buffalo Bill's Wild West revived in 1916. Tammen demanded $5,000 for the use of Buffalo Bill's name in the 1916 revival of Buffalo Bill's West. Cody still had hopes for his

Oracle mine, and there was talk of selling prints from the Rosa Bonheur painting. When winter arrived, however, he embarked on writing a series of articles for *Hearst's International* magazine. As had happened so many times in the past, they were published with much editing and in-house expansion. Beginning in August 1916, "The Great West That Was" series captivated fresh audiences and, following his death, was reprinted as his last autobiography.[37]

The era of the Wild West seemed curiously out of place in 1916. Most of Europe was at war, and the United States was finding it increasingly difficult to follow President Wilson's urging that she should "remain neutral in fact as well as in name." The sinking of the British R.M.S. *Lusitania* by a German U-boat in 1915 and the subsequent loss of lives, many of them American, left many citizens with a feeling that the time was fast approaching when the United States, too, would enter the conflict. As a result, a spate of "preparedness" campaigns spread across the nation. Buffalo Bill approached the chief of staff of the U.S. Army, Major General Hugh L. Scott, with an idea for a Pageant of Preparedness that could include a Wild West spectacle as well as troops and armament. The general willingly gave his approval, and Cody looked around for a backer and a suitable vehicle for his part of the spectacle.

The 101 Ranch Wild West was the

CODY *and General Scott at Fort Bliss, Texas, April 30, 1914, from a photograph* *by L. Moxie Manley of Kansas City, Missouri. (Courtesy Robert Pollock)*

most obvious choice, but it was in a semi-depressed state. The Miller Brothers who had created and toured with the show had chosen 1914 to tour Europe. When Great Britain and Germany went to war on August 4, 1914, the British government promptly pressed the majority of their stock into military service, and the company returned to the United States with only a few highly trained animals that would have been useless anywhere

but in the arena. The 1915 season had not been a success, despite the appearance of the Kansas cowboy, Jess Willard, who had turned boxer and knocked out Jack Johnson on April 5. Willard joined the Sells-Floto Circus in 1916; Tammen may have swapped him for Cody.[38]

As it turned out, Buffalo Bill did not achieve any share in the ownership of the pageant, but he did receive $100 a day

BUFFALO *Bill's friendship with General Hugh L. Scott gained him an introduction to many people. Here he and the general are* *talking to Mexican general Marcado at Fort Bliss, Texas, on April 30, 1914. (Courtesy Buffalo Bill Historical Center)*

and one-third of all profits over $2,750 daily. Russell reports that in one week he made $4,161.35. Billed as "Miller & Arlington Wild West Show Co., Inc., present 'Buffalo Bill' (himself) Combined with the 101 Ranch Shows," it included batteries of field guns and cavalry, together with a number of high-jumping horses, and several Arab and Japanese acrobats. But what really attracted audiences was the Wild West spectacle, which included erstwhile Cody-inspired Pony Express riding and other events associated with his original exhibition. Despite his comparatively minor role, Cody was happy; he rejoiced in having behind the scenes Johnny Baker and others whom he could trust. The performances

were always crowded, and for the first time in years, many were turned away.[39]

Russell gives an amusing account of how, because the residents of Chicago represented the "sixth German city in the world," the mayor insisted that the name of the show be changed from "preparedness" to the "Chicago Shan-Kive and Round-up" during its stay in the city that August. "Shan-Kive" apparently meant "a good time" and "round-up" meant "rodeo"—a little-known word at the time.[40]

As the season wore on, however, interest waned, and profits dropped. When Cody, who needed money, heard that holders of the Medal of Honor were eligible for pay, he wrote to the adjutant

BUFFALO *Bill the Magnifico, from a portrait, ca. 1915.*   *(Courtesy Hastings Museum)*

BUFFALO *Bill wearing eyeglasses to get a "spectacular" view of an early airplane, ca.* *1915. (Courtesy Buffalo Bill Historical Center)*

THE *loss of his son, Kit, was a source of great sorrow to Cody for the remainder of his life; but thanks to his daughters, he was blessed with grandchildren. This photograph, ca. 1915, shows the colonel and Lulu with two of them at North Platte. (Courtesy Buffalo Bill Historical Center)*

general on his show stationery. He requested ten dollars a month for "his business as it rains all the time." He had been misinformed; no money was paid. Furthermore, in 1913 *Army Regulations* had decreed that only enlisted men or officers were entitled to the medal. Cody's name had been struck from the record. As has been clarified elsewhere, Buffalo Bill did not lose his Congressional Medal of Honor, and shortly before his death he received a certificate confirming his entitlement both to the medal and to a place on the roll of honor.

The 1916 season proved to be the old scout's last. Despite an optimism that was staggering, his health had not been good. Several times he had had to be helped onto his horse behind the scenes and allowed to rest for a few minutes before he straightened his back, dug his heels in, and gallantly rode out to face his audience, who never ever suspected that anything was amiss. It has been stated that the final performance of the Wild West took place on November 4, 1916, but this is not so. The *Itinerary* reveals that it closed at Portsmouth, Virginia, on November 11. Some of those last engage-

ments have English resonances for the authors: Durham, Raleigh, and Plymouth in North Carolina and, on the very last day, Portsmouth, Virginia. It must be stated firmly that Cody had no intention of retiring after the Portsmouth engagement. Rather, he was already preparing for the 1917 season. First, he decided to visit his sister May in Denver before going on to Cody, where he planned to spend the winter and work on some more articles for Hearst.

By the time Cody reached May's home, however, he was mentally and physically exhausted. That last tour had taken a toll far greater than anyone had realized. May immediately sent for Louisa, Irma, and Cody's other sister, Julia. Their arrival seemed to revive the old scout, for within a few days he was up on his feet and headed for Wyoming. Reports that he planned to visit New York to raise fresh capital were premature. He returned to Denver, where once again his wife and his sisters revived him. Dr. J. P. East then suggested that perhaps a trip to Glenwood Springs to try the healing waters might help, so accompanied by the doctor and Julia he set off, while the others returned to Cody.

Buffalo Bill had withstood the journey, but he was so weakened that the doctor was convinced that he was dying. Julia and Dr. East took him back to Denver, and again the family was sent for. Louisa did not come because, as she later recalled, she had been assured by Cody

THE *last glimpse of Buffalo Bill, from a photograph taken at Glenwood Springs, Colorado, on January 6, 1917. C. E. Kreuger, of Glenwood Springs, captured this last image outside the stone bathhouse, surely an unromantic view of a man who belonged so completely to the wide-open spaces of the plains and the distant mountains. Cody himself seems almost aware of the historical significance of this, his last public appearance. (Courtesy Scout's Rest Ranch)*

himself that "I've still got my boots on. I'll be alright." By January 8, however, there was cause for concern. The telegraph wires across the country sang with the news that Buffalo Bill was near death. The news was greeted with disbelief by some, while others who had been close to him knew that it was only a matter of time. Hourly bulletins on his health were circulated, and Boy Scouts and others stood by in case they could be of any help to the family. On the ninth it was reported that Father Christopher V. Walsh—presumably at the insistence of Louisa—had baptized Cody into the Roman Catholic Church. However, according to one source, Louisa was an Episcopalian, while Cody had previously informed Julia, a Presbyterian, that "your church suits me."[41]

Reports that the old scout played cards during his last hours may have been exaggerated, but it seems clear that he did participate in a couple of hands of high five. His main concern, however, was

that Johnny Baker should get there in time. "I wish Johnny would come," he kept saying, and Johnny was doing his best. Broken-hearted, he was racing through the night by train from New York. But he was too late. At exactly five minutes past noon on January 10, 1917, Buffalo Bill died. Within minutes the news was telegraphed around the world, being given a "CLEAR THE LINE" status by Western Union and the other telegraph companies that at that time was usually reserved for war news.

Back in the United States, the White House reacted quickly; President Woodrow Wilson and generals Scott and Miles paid tribute to Cody's services as a scout in the Old West. From England came a message from King George V and Queen Mary. Condolences from heads of state and others from all over the world arrived. Indeed, for one day, William Frederick Cody stole the limelight from a world war.[42]

Then a fight began—to decide where the old scout should be buried. With the news of his death came a statement that he was to be buried on top of Lookout Mountain, above Denver. This statement shook his friends, for he had often stated that he wished to be buried on Cedar Mountain, in Wyoming, as his will had requested. Louisa, however, claims that with death very close he had declared, "I want to be buried on top of Mount Lookout. It's right over Denver. You can look down into four states there. It's pretty up

BUFFALO Bill's last resting place, atop Lookout Mountain near Denver. Every year thousands visit the grave of the man whose life and legend personifies the Old West. (Courtesy Scout's Rest Ranch) ABOVE

DURING his career as a dime-novel hero, Buffalo Bill was sketched by many artists. In England, the late Derek C. Eyles, a prolific illustrator of innumerable boys' books and comics, illustrated a series of stories about Buffalo Bill published in the early 1950s. These prints, made from his original drawings, show his attention to detail and the influence of Hollywood in his depiction of Cody as a scout-cum-gunfighter. (From the collection of Joseph G. Rosa) OPPOSITE

BUFFALO Bill's grandson dedicates a memorial plaque that celebrates the centennial of the first public performance of the Wild West at Earl's Court, London, on May 9, 1987. (Courtesy Alan Treweeke Enterprises, Ltd.)

there. I want to be buried up there—instead of Wyoming."[43]

Whether Cody really changed his mind, or as some cynics claimed, the evil Harry Tammen had changed Louisa's with a payment of $10,000 is now a moot point. The fact remains that Tammen was very much involved in the decision to bury Buffalo Bill on Lookout Mountain, and that is where he now rests, his grave a focal point for tourists and others drawn to the last resting place of the great scout. And for those of his family and friends who mourned him, death again took its toll in a short space of time. Irma and her husband, Fred Garlow, victims of influenza, died within a few days of each other in October 1918. Louisa died following a heart attack in October 1921, and Johnny Baker, who had loved Cody as a son would his own father, kept his idol's memory before the public for as long as he could. He died in a Denver hospital on April 22, 1931, and, at his own request, his ashes were taken to Rochester, New York, and buried near the graves of Arta, Orra, and Kit.[44]

Millions of children and those not so young who had worshiped Buffalo Bill either in person or as a dime-novel hero, mourned him. That he deserved his reputation as a scout, guide, hunter, and great showman is established by the record. That he was also guilty of sometimes stretching the truth if it suited him is not denied, but the fact remains that William Frederick Cody, alias Buffalo Bill, did more than any other individual to perpetuate the myth and the reality of the American West. He presented before the world an authentic spectacle of an era that in its way was an epic in world history. We are forever in his debt.

NOTES

1 *Daily Telegraph,* March 16, 1903.

2 Ibid.

3 *Manchester Evening News,* April 14 and 21, 1903.

4 *Wimbledon News,* June 25, 1904; *Itinerary.*

5 Don Russell, *The Lives and Legends of Buffalo Bill* (Norman, Okla., 1960; hereafter cited as Russell, *Lives*), 441.

6 Ibid., 443.

7 Ibid., 443–445.

8 Richard E. Conover, "Notes on the Barnum and Bailey Show," *Bandwagon* (March–April 1959).

9 Russell, *Lives,* 446–448; Glenn Shirley, *Pawnee Bill: A Biography of Major Gordon W. Lillie* (Albuquerque, 1958), 176–191.

10 Russell, *Lives,* 448–449.

11 Ibid., 450–451; Frank Winch, *Thrilling Lives of Buffalo Bill and Pawnee Bill* (New York, 1911), 217–224.

12 Nellie Snyder Yost, *Buffalo Bill: His Family, Friends, Failures, and Fortunes* (Chicago, 1979; hereafter cited as Yost, *Buffalo Bill*), 363.

13 Russell, *Lives,* 451.

14 Flagstaff, Arizona, *Cocontino Sun,* November 10, 1892.

15 Russell, *Lives,* 426.

16 Ibid., 427.

17 Ibid., 430–431.

18 "The Truth about Buffalo Bill" (A Symposium), *The Westerners Brand Book, 1945–46* (Chicago, 1947), 27–31; Russell, *Lives*, 431–432.

19 Russell, *Lives*, 435.

20 Ibid., 438.

21 Ibid., 453.

22 Gene Fowler, *Timberline: A Story of Bonfils and Tammen* (New York, 1933; hereafter cited as Fowler, *Timberline*), 38, 46–48, 86–89, 99, 373.

23 Ibid., 207–209.

24 Russell, *Lives*, 453.

25 *Denver Post*, February 5, 1913.

26 Fowler, *Timberline*, 377; Russell, *Lives*, 454; Paul Fees to Joseph G. Rosa, August 17, 1988. Dr. Fees kindly supplied a copy of the agreement, which is on file at the Buffalo Bill Historical Center. This document, dated January 28, 1913, makes it clear that Cody was "desirous of connecting himself" with the Sells-Floto Company, which gave Tammen the right to use the title Buffalo Bill's Wild West, or Buffalo Bill's Wild West and Congress of Rough Riders of the World, or "other names or titles as it may elect." It also declared that Cody would endeavor to make arrangements with Lillie to enable him to appear. Seventy-five years after it was drawn up, the agreement is still curious and confusing.

27 Russell, *Lives*, 455.

28 Ibid., 455; Yost, *Buffalo Bill; Itinerary.*

29 Russell, *Lives*, 455; Yost, *Buffalo Bill*, 384.

30 Fowler, *Timberline*, 377–378; Yost, *Buffalo Bill*, 384–385.

31 Fowler, *Timberline*, 378–379; Yost, *Buffalo Bill*, 386.

32 Russell, *Lives*, 456–457.

33 Ibid., 457; Yost, *Buffalo Bill*, 387–392.

34 Russell, *Lives*, 458; Yost, *Buffalo Bill*, 393.

35 Russell, *Lives*, 458–461; Stella Adelyne Foote, *Letters from "Buffalo Bill"* (Billings, Mont., 1954), 76; Richard J. Walsh, with Milton S. Salsbury, *The Making of Buffalo Bill* (Indianapolis, 1928), 351–352.

36 Russell, *Lives*, 460.

37 Ibid., 461–462.

38 Ibid., 463.

39 Ibid., 464.

40 Ibid., 464–465.

41 Ibid., 469; Yost, *Buffalo Bill,* 401.

42 Ibid.

43 Louisa Frederici Cody, in collaboration with Courtney Ryley Cooper, *Memories of Buffalo Bill* (New York and London, 1920), 324.

44 Yost, *Buffalo Bill,* 411–413.

BIBLIOGRAPHY

Books and Pamphlets

Adami, Giuseppe, ed. *Letters from Giacomo Puccini*. Philadelphia, 1931.

Armes, Col. George A. *Ups and Downs of an Army Officer*. Washington, D.C., 1900.

Blackstone, Sarah. *Buckskins, Bullets, and Business*. Westport, Conn., 1986.

Botkin, B. A., ed. *A Treasury of American Folklore*. New York, 1944.

Buffalo Bill's Wild West and Congress of Rough Riders of the World (1893 program). Chicago, 1893.

Churchill, Randolph. *Winston Churchill* (Vol. 1). London, 1966.

Cody, Louisa, in collaboration with Courtney Ryley Cooper. *Memories of Buffalo Bill*. New York and London, 1920.

Cody, W. F. *The Life of the Hon. William F. Cody, Known as Buffalo Bill, The Famous Hunter, Scout and Guide: An Autobiography*. Hartford, Conn., 1879.

———. *Story of the Wild West and Camp-Fire Chats*. Philadelphia, 1888.

Connelley, William E. *Wild Bill and His Era*. New York, 1933.

Cooper, Courtney Ryley. *Annie Oakley, Woman at Arms*. New York, 1927.

Custer, Gen. George A. *My Life on the Plains*. New York, 1876.

Danker, Donald F., ed. *Man of the Plains: Recollections of Luther North, 1856–1882*. Lincoln, Nebr., 1961.

Davies, Henry E. *Ten Days on the Plains*. New York, 1871.

Disher, M. Willson. *Greatest Show on Earth*. London, 1937.

Dunraven, The Earl of. *Canadian Nights*. New York, 1914.

Erskine, Gladys Shaw. *Broncho Charlie, A Saga of the Saddle: The Autobiography of Broncho Charlie Miller*. London, 1935.

Fellows, Dexter W., and Andrew A. Freeman. *This Way to the Big Show*. New York, 1936.

Flayderman, Norm. *Flayderman's Guide to Antique American Firearms and Their Values*. 3rd ed. Northfield, Ill., 1983.

Foote, Stella Adelyne. *Letters from "Buffalo Bill."* Billings, Mont., 1954.

Foreman, Carolyn Thomas. *Indians Abroad*. Norman, Okla., 1943.

Fowler, Gene. *Timberline: A Story of Bonfils and Tammen*. New York, 1933.

Furnas, J. C. *The Americans: A Social History of the United States, 1587–1914*. London, 1969.

Havinghurst, Walter. *Annie Oakley of the Wild West*. New York, 1954.

Howard, J. W. ("Doc"). *"Doc" Howard's Memoirs*. Denver, Colo., ca. 1931.

Hutton, Paul Andrew. *Phil Sheridan and His Army*. Lincoln, Nebr., and London, 1985.

Irving, Laurence. *Henry Irving*. London, 1951.

Johansen, Albert. *The House of Beadle and Adams and Its Dime and Nickel Novels: The Story of a Vanished Literature*. Norman, Okla., 1950.

Lamar, Howard R., ed. *The Reader's Encyclopedia of the American West*. New York, 1977.

Leonard, Elizabeth Jane, and Julia Cody Goodman. *Buffalo Bill: King of the Old West*. New York, 1955.

Logan, Herschel C. *Buckskin and Satin*. Harrisburg, Pa., 1954.

Longford, Elizabeth. *Queen Victoria*. London, 1964.

McCoy, Col. Tim, and Ronald McCoy. *Tim McCoy Remembers the Wild West*. New York, 1977.

McLaughlin, James. *My Friend the Indian*. Boston, New York, and London, 1926.

Majors, Alexander. *Seventy Years on the Frontier*. Chicago, 1893.

Miles, Gen. Nelson A. *Serving the Republic*. Chicago and New York, 1896.

Morison, Samuel Eliot, Henry Steele Commager, and William E. Leuchtenburg, *The Growth of the American Republic* (Vol. 1). London, 1980.

Neihardt, John G. (as told to). *Black Elk Speaks*. New York, 1932.

Nelson, John Young. *Fifty Years on the Trail: The Adventures of John Young Nelson, as Described to Harrington O'Reilly*. Norman, Okla., 1963.

Otero, Miguel Antonio. *My Life on the Frontier* (Vol. 1—1864–1882). New York, 1935.

Parsons, John E. *The Peacemaker and Its Rivals*. New York, 1950.

———. *Smith & Wesson Revolvers: The Pioneer Single Action Models*. New York, 1957.

Reader, W. J. *Life in Victorian England*. London, 1964.

Riley, James Francis. *Recollections of James Francis Riley (1838–1918)*. Independence, Mo., 1959.

Rosa, Joseph G. *They Called Him Wild Bill: The Life and Adventures of James Butler Hickok*. Norman, Okla., 1964 and 1974.

Russell, Don. *The Lives and Legends of Buffalo Bill*. Norman, Okla., 1960.

Sanger, "Lord" George. *Seventy Years a Showman*. London, 1927.

Savage, William W., Jr., ed. *Cowboy Life*. Norman, Okla., 1975.

Schuchert, Charles, and Clara Mae LeVene. *O. C. Marsh, Pioneer in Paleontology*. New Haven, Conn., 1940.

Secrest, William B., ed. *I Buried Hickok: The Memoirs of White Eye Anderson*. College Station, Tex., 1980.

Sheridan, Gen. Philip H. *Personal Memoirs* (2 vols.). New York, 1888.

Shirley, Glenn. *Pawnee Bill: A Biography of Major Gordon W. Lillie*. Albuquerque, 1958.

Spring, Agnes Wright. *The Cheyenne and Black Hills Stage and Express Routes*. Glendale, Calif., 1949.

Swartwout, Annie Fern. *Missie*. Blanchester, Ohio, 1947.

Taubman, Howard. *The Making of the American Theater*. New York, 1965.

Thorp, Raymond W. *Spirit Gun of the West: The Story of Doc W. F. Carver.* Glendale, Calif., 1957.

Time-Life Books. *The End and the Myth.* New York, 1979.

Turner, John Peter. *The North-West Mounted Police.* Ottawa, Ont., 1950.

Utley, Robert M. *Frontier Regulars.* New York, 1973.

———, ed. *Life in Custer's Cavalry: Diaries and Letters of Albert and Jennie Barnitz, 1867–1868.* New Haven, Conn., and London, 1977.

Vestal, Stanley. *Sitting Bull: Champion of the Sioux.* Norman, Okla., 1957.

Walker, Henry Pickering. *The Wagonmasters.* Norman, Okla., 1966.

Wallace, Irving, *The Fabulous Showman.* London, 1960.

Walsh, Richard J., with Milton S. Salsbury. *The Making of Buffalo Bill.* Indianapolis, 1928.

Webb, William E. *Buffalo Land.* Cincinnati and Chicago, 1872.

The Westerners Brand Book (1945–46). Chicago, 1947.

Wetmore, Helen Cody. *The Last of the Great Scouts: The Life of Col. W. F. Cody "Buffalo Bill."* London, 1901.

Williams, Robert H. *With the Border Ruffians: Memories of the Far West 1852–1868.* London, 1907.

Williamson, Harold F. *Winchester: The Gun That Won the West.* New York, 1978.

Winch, Frank. *Thrilling Lives of Buffalo Bill and Pawnee Bill.* New York, 1911.

Yost, Nellie Snyder. *Buffalo Bill: His Family, Friends, Failures, and Fortunes.* Chicago, 1979.

Zurhurst, Charles. *The First Cowboy.* New York, 1973.

Magazines and Articles

Almy, Kenneth J., ed. "Thof's Dragon and the Letters of Capt. Theophilus H. Turner, M.D., U.S. Army," *Kansas History: A Journal of the Central Plains* 10, no. 3 (Autumn 1987): 185–186.

Cahill, Luke. "An Indian Campaign and Buffalo Hunting with 'Buffalo Bill,' " *Colorado Magazine* 4, no. 4 (August 1927).

Coleman, William S. E. "Buffalo Bill on Stage," *Players,* n.d.

Conover, Richard. "Notes on the Barnum and Bailey Show," *Bandwagon,* March–April 1959.

Deahl, William E., Jr. "Buffalo Bill's Wild West Show, 1885," *Annals of Wyoming* 47, no. 3 (Fall 1975).

Gray, John S. "Fact versus Fiction in the Kansas Boyhood of Buffalo Bill," *Kansas History* 8, no. 1 (Spring 1985).

———. "Will Comstock—The Natty Bumppo of Kansas," *The Westerners Brandbook* (Chicago) 18, no. 12 (February 1962).

Hanson, George W. "True Story of Wild Bill-McCanles Affray in Jefferson County, Nebraska, July 12, 1861" (with supporting articles by Addison E. Sheldon and William Monroe McCanles), *Nebraska History Magazine* 10, no. 2 (April–June 1927).

Lecompte, Janet. "Charles Autobees," *Colorado Magazine* 34, no. 3 (July 1957).

Montgomery, Mrs. Frank C. "Fort Wallace and Its Relation to the Frontier," Kansas State Historical Society *Collections* 17 (1926–28).

Moses, L. G. "Wild West Shows, Reformers and the Image of the American Indian, 1887–1914," *South Dakota History* 4, no. 3 (Fall 1984).

Nichols, Col. George Ward. "Wild Bill," *Harper's New Monthly Magazine* 24, no. 201 (February 1867).

Nordin, Charles R. "Dr. W. F. Carver, 'Evil Spirit of the Plains,'" *Nebraska History Magazine* 10, no. 4 (October–December 1927).

"Rare Recording by Buffalo Bill Is Given to the Library of Congress," *Library of Congress Information Bulletin* 41, no. 11 (March 12, 1982).

Remington, Frederic. "Buffalo Bill in London," *Harper's Weekly,* September 3, 1892.

Robbins, Hiram. "Wild Bill's Humors," *The Arkansaw Traveler.* n.d.

Rosa, Joseph G. "J. B. Hickok, Deputy U.S. Marshal," *Kansas History* 2, no. 4 (Winter 1979).

Russell, Don. "Julia Goodman's Memoirs of Buffalo Bill," *Kansas Historical Quarterly* 28, no. 4 (Winter 1962).

Salsbury, Nate. "The Origin of the Wild West Show," *Colorado Magazine* 32, no. 3 (July 1955).

Newspapers

The following newspapers were checked at random for the years 1854–1917 and are, therefore, listed by title rather than date.

Abilene, Kans., *Chronicle*
Baltimore, Md., *Daily American*
Boston, Mass., *Evening Transcript*
Chicago, Ill., *Daily Tribune*
Chicago, Ill., *Evening Journal*
Chicago, Ill., *Times*
Denver, Colo., *Evening Post*
Denver, Colo., *Post*
Denver, Colo., *Rocky Mountain News*
Ellis County, Kans., *Star*
Flagstaff, Ariz., *Cocontino Sun*
Fresno, Calif., *Daily Expositor*
Hays, Kans., *Republican*
Hays City, Kans., *Railway Advance*
Jefferson City, Mo., *People's Tribune*
Junction City, Kans., *Weekly Union*
Keokuk, Iowa, *Daily Gate City*
Lawrence, Kans., *Kansas Weekly Tribune*
Leavenworth, Kans., *Daily Conservative*
Leavenworth, Kans., *Daily Times*
Leavenworth, Kans., *Leavenworth Times*
Leavenworth, Kans., *Times and Conservative*
Liberty, Mo., *Democratic Platform*
London, England, *Daily Telegraph*
London, England, *Illustrated London News*
London, England, *Times*
Manchester, England, *Evening News*
Mendota, Ill., *Bulletin*

Milwaukee, Wis., *Sentinel*
Nebraska City, Nebr., *News-Press*
New Orleans, La., *Daily Picayune*
New York, *Daily Graphic*
New York Weekly
Omaha, Nebr., *Daily Bee*
Omaha, Nebr., *Daily Herald*
Pueblo, Colo., *Chieftain*
Rochester, N.Y., *Democrat and Chronicle*
St. Louis, Mo., *Globe Democrat*
St. Louis, Mo., *Missouri Democrat*
San Francisco, Calif., *Call*
Springfield, Mass., *Daily Republican*
Topeka, Kans., *Daily Commonwealth*
Waterville, Kans., *Telegraph*
Wimbledon, England, *Wimbledon News*

Manuscripts and Official Records

Carr, Gen. E. A. "Carr's Campaign of 1868–69." Ms. supplied by Prof. James T. King.

Carr, Brev. Maj. Gen. E. A. "Official Report of the 1868–69 Winter Campaign." Department of the Missouri, Letters Received, Record Group no. 343, National Archives, Washington, D.C.

Cody, W. F., to Henry A. Ward, November 29, 1882. University of Rochester Library, Rochester, N.Y.

Cody Scrapbooks, Buffalo Bill Historical Center, Cody, Wyo.

Hickok, Lorenzo Butler, to Polly Butler Hickok, December 2, 1867. Manuscripts Department, Kansas State Historical Society (KSHS), Topeka.

Itinerary of the Wild West (1883–1913). Buffalo Bill Historical Center, Cody, Wyo.

Kansas Tract Books, Vol. 16. Microfilm copy, Archives Department, KSHS.

Queen Victoria's Journal (1887 and 1892). The Royal Archives, Windsor Castle.

Records of the Department of the Platte, Omaha, Nebr., National Archives, Washington, D.C.

Records of Persons Hired by the Quartermaster General (1861–1876), National Archives, Washington, D.C.

Records of Fort Hays, Kansas (Letters Dispatched 1867). Microfilm copy, Manuscripts Department, KSHS.

Records of Fort Hays, Kansas (Letters Received 1868). Microfilm copy, Manuscripts Department, KSHS.

Records of the Office of the Pardon Attorney, No. F-307 (John alias Jack McCall) Records Group no. 24, National Archives, Washington, D.C.

Records of the Seventh Kansas Volunteer Cavalry Regiment, Archives Division, KSHS.

INDEX